TITLE:	"---Nobody can say---we didn't have a---lot---of music---"
	He finishes and continues:
TITLE:	"---such as it is!---"
	He finishes - she nods - CAMERA MOVES BACK - they walk to door.
M L S	Couryard - Dragoons mounted - Nicki's horse waiting - Nicki and Mitzi enter from left - he kisses her hands - then goes to horse - as he fixes his bridle and examines the cinch - she comes slowly up to him - she has still her apple blossom branche in arm.
M S U	Both in - she breaks off a twig - kisses it - holds it out to Nicki - he takes it - kisses it reverently - puts it in his left coat pocket - she opens once more her arms - he kisses her.
STOCK	SHOT OF GUNS FIRING.
B T M L S	He breaks - then mounts - she waves to him - he draws sword - salutes her - Nicki rides to the head of the column - then rides out.
M L S	Front of Convent wall - Nicki leads Dragoons out.
M C U	Trumpeters blowing Cavalry Marching signal.
B T	Couryard - Mitzi stands there looking after soldiers - then turns to door - quickly runs in.
L S	Convent - Dragoons trot~~~~~~ ~~~~~~ toward ~~~~~~ - Artillery and trucks pass.
STOCK	SHOT OF GUNS BOOMING.
M S	TOWER TOP - Mitzi enters in great haste - she looks down toward bridge.
B T L S	Dragoons ride over bridge and disappear.
M C U	Mitzi - tears are rolling down her cheeks - she waves sub- consciously - then she folds her hands and prays with face toward Heaven.
STOCK	SHOT OF GUNS BOOMING.
	FADE OUT.

Works of art are of an infinite loneliness,
and with nothing to be so little reached as
with criticism. Only love can grasp and
hold and fairly judge them.

— *Rilke*

Archetypical waltz of pre–World War I Vienna, the "Old Vienna" of song and story

—Johann Strauss
Thousand and One Nights, Solomon's Song, Act I

Fortune smiles once more on me from above,
Returning the woman that I do so love.
How I did miss you —
How I did yearn —
Sweet is the moment that sees your return!

A fool is he who lets his chance pass him by,
Unworthy of all that Love makes lovers sigh. . . .

THE AMERICAN FILM INSTITUTE SERIES

Books by Herman G. Weinberg

Josef Von Sternberg
The Lubitsch Touch
Saint Cinema
The Complete "Greed"
The Complete Wedding March *of Erich von Stroheim*

THE COMPLETE WEDDING MARCH

THE COMPLETE
WEDDING MARCH
OF ERICH VON STROHEIM

A RECONSTRUCTION OF THE FILM,
PART ONE, "THE WEDDING MARCH," PART TWO, "THE HONEYMOON,"
IN 255 STILL PHOTOS FOLLOWING THE ORIGINAL SCREENPLAY,
PLUS 13 PRODUCTION STILLS

COMPILED AND ANNOTATED
WITH A FOREWORD BY

HERMAN G. WEINBERG

FOR THE AMERICAN FILM INSTITUTE

LITTLE, BROWN AND COMPANY - BOSTON - TORONTO

First Edition

T 01/75

Endleaves: the first and last pages of the original shooting copy of *The Complete Wedding March.*

LIBRARY OF CONGRESS CATALOGING IN PUBLICATION DATA

Von Stroheim, Erich, 1885–1957.
  The complete Wedding march of Erich von Stroheim.

  I. Weinberg, Herman G.   II.   Wedding march.
[Motion picture]   III.   Title.
PN1997.W414V6   791.43'7   74-16283
ISBN 0-316-92842-9

Designed by Barbara Bell Pitnof

*Published simultaneously in Canada
by Little, Brown & Company (Canada) Limited*

Printed in the United States of America

ACKNOWLEDGMENTS

The author is grateful for permission to quote material from the following previously published works:

Grierson on Documentary, edited and with an Introduction by Forsyth Hardy. Copyright © 1946 and 1966 by John Grierson. Excerpted and reprinted by permission of Praeger Publishers, Inc., New York, and Faber & Faber, Ltd., London.

Kafka and Prague, text by Johann Bauer. Quotation from Ignat Herrmann reprinted by permission of The Pall Mall Press Ltd, London. Quotation from Franz Kafka's letter to his sister, Ottla, reprinted by permission of Schocken Books, Inc., New York. Copyright © 1971 by Chr. Belser Verlag, Stuttgart, Germany. Excerpts reprinted by permission of Praeger Publishers, New York, London.

Erich von Stroheim by Freddy Buache. "La Symphonie Nuptiale." *Cinéma d'Aujourd'hui,* No. 71. Copyright © Éditions Seghers, Paris, 1972. Reprinted by permission.

Strauss-Reiterer: 1001 Nacht, Walzerlied no. 10 (Solomon's Song, Act 1, "Thousand and One Nights"). Copyright © Aug. Cranz, GmbH., Musik Verlag, Wiesbaden, and excerpted by permission.

Etudes cinématographiques, 48–50, "Stroheim" by Denis Marion and Barthélemy Amengual. Excerpts from "Stroheim entre la legende et l'histoire" by Barthélemy Amengual and from an *hommage* by Jean Renoir. Copyright © Lettres Modernes, Paris, 1966 and excerpted and reprinted by permission.

Stroheim by Joel W. Finler, copyright © Movie Magazine Ltd. 1967, London, published by Studio Vista Ltd., London. Excerpted and reprinted by permission.

Wittgenstein's Vienna by Allan Janik and Stephen Toulmin. Copyright © 1973. Excerpted and reprinted by permission of Simon and Schuster, New York (publisher).

Anatol: A Sequence of Dialogues by Arthur Schnitzler, paraphrased for the English stage by Granville Barker. Excerpt from the preface. Copyright © 1917 by Little, Brown & Co., Boston, and reprinted by permission.

Recollections of Virginia Woolf by Her Contemporaries. Edited by John Russell Noble. Rebecca West excerpt. Copyright © William Morrow & Company, Inc., New York, 1973. Reprinted by permission.

Gold and Silver: The Life and Times of Franz Lehár by Bernard Grunn. Copyright © 1970 by Bernard Grunn. Excerpted and reprinted by permission of the publishers, David McKay Company, Inc., New York.

1913: An End and a Beginning by Virginia Cowles, pp. 140, 141, 154, 155. Copyright © 1967 by Crawley Features. Reprinted by permission of Harper & Row, Publishers, Inc., New York.

The Hapsburg Curse by Hans Holzer. Copyright © 1973 by Hans Holzer. Excerpted and reprinted by permission of Doubleday and Company, Inc., New York.

The American Cinema: Directors and Directions (1929–1968) by Andrew Sarris. Copyright © 1968 by Andrew Sarris. Excerpted and reprinted by permission of E. P. Dutton & Co., New York.

Josef von Sternberg: A Critical Study by Herman G. Weinberg. Copyright © 1967 by Herman G. Weinberg. Excerpted and reprinted by permission of E. P. Dutton & Co., New York.

Anatol, Living Hours, The Green Cockatoo by Arthur Schnitzler. Introduction by Ashley Dukes. Copyright © 1917 by Boni & Liveright, New York.

Unholy Fools: Wits, Comics and Disturbers of the Peace by Penelope Gilliatt. Copyright © 1973 by Penelope Gilliatt. Excerpted and reprinted by permission of Viking Press, Publishers, New York.

The Journal of Jules Renard, edited and translated by Louise Bogan and Elizabeth Roget. George Braziller, New York, copyright © 1964. Excerpted and reprinted by permission of the publisher.

Von Stroheim: A Symposium. A letter from Denise Vernac to Giulio Cesare Castello on *La Dame Blanche.* Copy-

The author is additionally grateful to the following individuals for their help in making this book possible: Dr. Peter Marboe of the Austrian Consulate in New York for checking the historical accuracy of the foreword, Ulf Pacher, also of the Austrian Consulate, Richard Watts, Pierre Sauvage, Mischa Delman, Marcello Maestro, Mario Maestro, Freddy Buache of the Cinémathèque Suisse, Audrey Kupferberg, William Kenly, Charles Hofmann, Arthur Kleiner, Eugenie Whitaker, Richard Sickinger of the Austrian Cultural Institute in New York, Dr. Ludwig Gesek of the Österreichische Gesellschaft für Filmwissenschaft of Vienna, Joseph Wechsberg, Jon Barna, Paul Falkenberg, Frederick Ungar, finally Elisabeth Gleason Humez for checking the manuscript, which took the patience of a saint, Barbara Pitnof, for employing the witchery of a sorceress in designing the book, and Sali Ann Kriegsman, of the American Film Institute, who was catalyst for the whole project.

This is a love-letter to a film.

And a true love-letter is full of kisses.

But, Kafka reminds us, ''. . . to write a love-letter means to strip one's self for the benefit of ghosts who are waiting eagerly for just this. Kisses that are written down do not reach their destination — the ghosts drink them on the way.''

But as I have put in so many, maybe they will not have drunk them all. Maybe some will be left for the reader in these pages.

—H. G. W.

O swallow, swallow, flying south,
Fly to her and rest upon her eaves
And tell her, tell her what I tell to thee. . . .
. . . Brief is life but love is long,
. . . And tell her, tell her that I follow thee!

— *after Tennyson*

To Gretchen

CONTENTS

FOREWORD

Remembrance holds the secret of redemption.
— Baal Shem Tov

Rossini, when asked who, for him, was the greatest of composers, unhesitatingly replied, "Beethoven."

"And Mozart?" he was asked.

"You said 'greatest,'" he answered. "You didn't say 'unique.'"

If I were asked to name the greatest film director, I would as unhesitatingly reply, "Eisenstein."

And if my interrogator persisted with "And Chaplin?" I, too, would answer, "You said 'greatest'; you didn't say 'unique.'"

Or I could just as well have named Griffith to such a query, just as Rossini could have named Bach, and, if my questioner came back with, "And von Stroheim?" have similarly answered, "You said 'greatest'; you didn't say 'unique.'"

In any case, these are for me the four Olympians on the film Parnassus and this is a book about one of them, perhaps in his own way (always excepting Chaplin, of course) unique among directors, using a work of his deepest maturity and reflection, *The Wedding March,* to show this.

Of course he had said that only *Greed* was his most fully realized work, that only *Greed* had total validity, but that was because only *Greed* existed, once, briefly, as a fully realized film for him, in its complete original form. And that was the film he referred to. He did not "recognize" the cut version released. *The Wedding March* remained unfinished (I almost said "was destined to remain unfinished" and that would have been correct, too) — it was never permitted to be a fully realized work, filming having been stopped at about two-thirds of the way into what was subsequently to become the second part of a two-part film, the reason being its financial backer P. A. Powers's sudden panic that Stroheim had gone a half million dollars over budget (of $700,000) with the end seemingly nowhere in sight. Even with the last third of the film missing, Stroheim felt he could "round out" an ending in the editing that would still be true to the film. But no one ever saw his first rough cut of 50,000 feet (eleven hours) which he had reduced from the approximately 200,000 feet shot, nor did anyone see the first cuts of Part One of 25,795 feet nor the 22,484 feet of Part Two.* Ultimately Part One was released worldwide by Paramount (to whom Powers had ceded the rights for distribution in mid-production, just as the Goldwyn Company ceded its rights to *Greed* to Metro in mid-production when the two companies merged into Metro Goldwyn) in 10,852 feet (slightly under two hours) and Part Two in South America and Europe in a "version" of some 7,000 feet, of which about 2,000 comprised a "condensation" of Part One, to make the unfinished Part Two appear as a "separate whole film, complete in itself."

"As you can see," he once said, "I am not easily discouraged." He certainly wasn't.

*He had decided to cut the film into two parts when he realized he would not be permitted to have his complete film because of its inordinate length. Thus, the two parts would be shown either on succeeding nights or separately as independent films. Griffith had attempted the same thing before, in 1916 with *Intolerance,* which Lillian Gish said originally ran eight hours and was planned by Griffith to be shown on two separate nights in two parts of four hours each, with a dinner intermission each night — exactly what Stroheim wanted to do, first with *Greed,* then with *The Wedding March.* Eventually, Griffith was forced by the economics of film industry distribution to cut *Intolerance* down to under four hours.

When you think that only his first two films were presented close to what he wanted them to be and that, following *Blind Husbands* and *The Devil's Passkey*, his *Foolish Wives* was severely censored and reduced from its original conception, *Merry Go Round* was taken away from him and given to another director to finish, which resulted in a complete watering down of his original intention, *Greed* was reduced to a quarter of its original length, the dark wine of *The Merry Widow* was adulterated with a banal happy ending and the excision of all its more "gamey" passages from the witty paraphrase he and Benjamin Glazer concocted from the original libretto, you have to admire the persistence of the man in again exposing enough film (for *The Wedding March*) to "girdle the earth," knowing, as he must have known by then, that he was heading for trouble. And as if that still was insufficient to prove that "the wall is harder than the head," after his fifth unhappy experience in a row, he came up from the "floor of the ring" (which was getting to be a familiar place to him), head bloodied but unbowed, game to try again. This time, with *Queen Kelly*, he not only went through half the total $800,000 budget up to the one-fourth point in the story, which, in effect, constituted just the prologue, but became the victim of a new exasperation, the advent of the sound film, which suddenly made all silent films obsolete. So production was again halted, and only an unedited fragment of the film remained. Remaining also was a last desperate attempt to "rehabilitate" himself from the stigma as the screen's most

"recalcitrant" director, one "who could not be managed." This he accomplished with *Walking Down Broadway*, his first sound film, brought in within the scheduled shooting time and *under* budget (and a modest budget at that), only to find himself upon completion of the film in the crossfire of a feud between two studio moguls which ended again in his being fired and his film being taken away from him and not just recut this time but remade. This was the end. He never directed another film. One looks back at these seven *"films maudits"* and sees again in the mind's eye the troubled beauty that were these seven, mystical seven — reverence to this.

Thirty-six different sets were designed by the director and his aide, ex-British army Captain Richard Day, for *The Wedding March*, and built at the Associated Studios, owned by the film's backer, P. A. Powers, where the picture was shot. Included were the façade and nave of St. Stephen's Cathedral with the Stefansplatz around it, the byways and wine-gardens of Nussdorf in the suburbs, and other *endroits* of urban and suburban Vienna. I remember reading about Stroheim's walking through the sets with Captain Day murmuring, "This is it . . . this is Vienna . . . *my* Vienna!" In truth he had a great affection for this film, not only because he was making live again the vanished Vienna of his youth, before the first World War, that holocaust which had brought the proud Austrian capital to its knees, but because it was, as *Greed* before that had been for him, another dream come true: another chance to make the film he was forbidden to make in

Merry Go Round five years earlier, his first attempt at a film about his native heath— alt Wien—Old Vienna.

"*Bella gerant alii, tu, felix Austria, nube. Nam quae Mars aliis, dat tibi regna Venus.*" "Let others make wars, you, happy Austria, marry. For Venus gives kingdoms to you as Mars gives them to others." (The Hapsburgs were collateral descendants through intermarriage of the sixteenth-century royal house of Spain—Charles V, Philip II, etc.—from whence derived their formal court etiquette.) This paraphrase of Ovid became the "motto" of the House of Hapsburg beginning with Maximilian I, whose marriage to Mary of Burgundy in 1477 and subsequent dynastic marriages of convenience secured for his successors one of the largest empires in history, including the Low Countries, the Spanish empire, Austria, Bohemia, Hungary and, of course, Burgundy. "Let others make films about gay old Vienna," said Stroheim; "I will make films about sad old Vienna, not because Vienna is sadder than any other city but because the world is sad." ("Not only Prague, but the whole world is tragic," said Kafka before him.)

And so Stroheim made not only the first notable film of Vienna (*Merry Go Round,* begun in 1922), but also the first sad film of Vienna. And though he wasn't permitted to finish it, it cast its spell of gray melancholy not only over that portion completed by Rupert Julian, who succeeded him as director, but over such notable subsequent meditations on the old city by the Danube as Pabst's *Joyless Street,* a thing of deep shadows and pale dis-

traught faces of a famine-stricken Vienna during the inflation, made unutterably forlorn in the glare of white light; Ophuls's *Liebelei,* after the incisive Schnitzler story, a coldly clinical study of the pitfalls of playing with love; Sternberg's *The Case of Lena Smith,* that harsh examination of Austrian Junkerism in the so-called "good old days" of Franz Josef I, and his *Dishonored,* in which Ivanovici's tinkling little "Danube Waves" waltz becomes a *Totentanz,* a dance of death; Anatole Litvak's *Mayerling,* that somber retelling of the Archduke Rudolph–Maria Vetsera idyll that ended with two shots; finally Ophuls's *Letter from an Unknown Woman* and *La Ronde,* the former after the desolate Stefan Zweig romance, the latter after Schnitzler's cynical "daisy chain," *Reigen,* that acrid sexual roundelay which, in the guise of a series of bleakly wry dialogues (read: couplings), was "stripped of the romance of *Anatol,*" as Ashley Dukes put it, "and reduced to a vivisection of the sex instinct, a post-mortem examination of passion . . . the work of an artist weary of many adventures, and disposed to regard life as nothing but a round of stupid intrigue and cynical reaction." Surely Ophuls came as close as Pabst and Sternberg in their best moments did to depths first plumbed by Stroheim in his (Ophuls's) trilogy of Vienna: *Liebelei, Letter from an Unknown Woman* and *La Ronde.* Andrew Sarris has put it acutely in describing "the desperate effort of Wolfgang Liebeneiner in *Liebelei* to recapture his lost innocence with Magda Schneider on a sleigh ride that is mystically reprised by the camera after they have both died. It is not merely the moving camera that expresses the tragedy of lost illusions, but the preciseness of the playing. There is a direct link between Liebeneiner and Gérard Philipe's jaded Count in *La Ronde* looking deep into Simone Signoret's eyes to find something he has forgotten forever. There is the same delicacy of regret nearly twenty years apart."*

Again seven, mystical seven . . . seven threnodies on the theme of Vienna in a somber mood. Stroheim's own trilogy on this theme comprised *Merry Go Round*, *The Wedding March* and *La Dame Blanche*, the first being only partially his, even though his intention permeated the whole film, so vital was the impulse that actuated it, while the last remained only in script form, its production cut off by the outbreak of World War II. Remained, then, only one almost completed film, *The Wedding March*, which, even in its truncated form, the only form in which anyone ever saw it (including the brief distribution abroad of what was put out as Part Two), still managed, as all these years the truncated *Greed* managed, to look like a Stroheim film. An evocation of the feudal strut of a vanished age, laced with the eternal eros of life.

Of course there was an obverse side to the coin of the Vienna mintage, too—the lighter side. A half dozen or so such bon-bons remain vivid and ineradicable in the memory after all these years—the years that separate us from them—caprices of giggling amorettes all tipped with their creators' names as women's hats with veils might be on display in a boutique window or at a modiste's shop: Lubitsch's *The Marriage Circle*, Ludwig Berger's *A Waltz Dream* and *Walzerkrieg*, the Erik Charell–Erich Pommer *The Congress Dances*, von Bolvary's *Two Hearts in Three-Quarter Time* and *The Merry Wives of Vienna*, Willy Forst's *Maskerade* and Walter Reisch's *Episode*—variations on the theme of Vienna as the city of "lights o' love," or waltzes as the beginning and end-all, but at least two, *The Marriage Circle* and *Maskerade*, with edges as cutting as their less facetious counterparts.

The characters who quickened this world—which seemed to have been one of eternal skirmish between the sexes, each vying for the upper hand—like the Schnitzler heroes and heroines, "have most of the vices of their city," again as Mr. Dukes puts it,* "and the quintessence of its charm, frivolity tinged with regret, and intrigue with grace."

These fifteen, then, as the ones that celebrated most notably, along with those with long and cherished memories, whatever to each was meant by *Alt Wien*, Old Vienna, "for better or for worse, in sickness and in health, till death do us part . . ."

The French, with their propensity for *le mot juste*, called *The Wedding March La Symphonie Nuptiale* ("The Wedding Symphony"), and the Italians (to whom France has always been *nostra sorella*, "our sister") followed suit with *Sinfonia Nuziale* and, in truth, that is exactly what it is, a film symphony on the

---

*Andrew Sarris, *The American Cinema: Directors and Directions, 1929–1968*, E. P. Dutton & Co., 1968.

*Arthur Schnitzler, *Anatol, Living Hours, The Green Cockatoo*, introduction by Ashley Dukes, Boni & Liveright, 1917.

theme of marriage (did not Richard Strauss write "A Domestic Symphony"?) in two broad movements composed of many motifs, a work of grand *ampleur,* which the musical accompaniment synchronized to the film on the sound track underscores. It is, in fact, a high mass, a requiem for a vanished world, a meditation on the theme of lost love.

But stay....

Note that, of the fifteen, only two have elements of fantasy in them — the others being played straight, realistically, whether for tragic or comic effect.

Which two?

The two by Stroheim, *The Wedding March* and *La Dame Blanche* — the mythical "Iron Man" of the former and the equally mythical "White Lady" of the latter. The "Iron Man," who sometimes came down from his perch atop the old Rathaus on troubled moonless eves and fished among the Danube naiads for one of the sprites, struggling in his arms, whom he carried back with him. To see this was an omen of bad luck, bringing "sorrow, grief and death," as poor Mitzi says in the film. The "White Lady," a wraith that floated through the palace at Schönbrunn on the eve of a tragedy for the Hapsburgs, was first "seen" in the modern era on the eve of the execution by the soldiers of Juárez, in Mexico, of the Emperor's ill-fated brother, Maximilian (it was Napoleon III's bright idea for Maximilian to crown himself Emperor of Mexico and Maximilian's wife, Carlotta, subsequently went mad from grief). She was next seen on the eve of the mysterious "double suicide" of the Emperor's son, Archduke Rudolph, and his mistress, Maria Vetsera, at his hunting lodge at Mayerling, and again before the assassination of the Emperor's wife, Empress Elizabeth, by an Italian anarchist in Geneva. Finally she appeared before the assassination of the Emperor's great-nephew, Archduke Ferdinand, and his wife at Sarajevo, which precipitated the first World War. In the case of the last, the White Lady floated out of the palace, so the legend went, and was visible as a diaphanous white mist, a marmoreal hoarfrost, floating over the city of Vienna, for this was an omen of tragedy not only for the Hapsburg dynasty, now coming to an end after a thousand years (the family could be traced back to the tenth century), but for Austria, and the dual monarchy, also coming to an end.

"Terrible, terrible!" the old Emperor was said to have cried when his ministers brought him the declaration of war against Serbia to sign, "No sorrow is spared me!" (Stroheim had this scene in *Merry Go Round*). Soon the nations of Europe were tumbling pell-mell, one after the other, into the maelstrom, with Austria first of the Central Powers to be crushed and ignominiously defeated and brought to the brink of disaster, utter and complete. But for all the misfortunes that overtook *den Alten,* "the old boy," as he was affectionately called by the populace, the *"Gott erhalte Franz den Kaiser"* of the country's national anthem worked. God *did* "hold him in the palm of His hand" for eighty-six years and gave him an equally long reign of sixty-eight years.

For some time, now, a dry rot had been setting in—the dual monarchy of Austro-Hungary being "supported" by a rebellious serfdom, the so-called minority, the vassal states comprising the Czechs, Slovaks, Bohemians, Poles, Serbs, and so on who were heavily taxed and exploited to support a top-heavy autocracy, the most authoritarian empire in Europe. The assassination of the Archduke Franz Ferdinand of Austria at Sarajevo (a visit of state that was to remind the obstreperous Serbs who was running things) was the lancing of an abscess which had long been forming on the body of the Hapsburg kingdom. The rebellious spirit had finally burst out. "If there had not been a war, there would surely have been a revolution." Only to the advisers, political and military, of Franz Josef and Wilhelm II of Germany, could such a thought originate as justification enough to be acted upon. Thus war became the lesser of two evils, the war for which the generals of the two Central Powers had long been champing at the bit. . . .

The war that lasted from 1914 to 1918 was certainly no fantasy but the Iron Man of *The Wedding March* was just as certainly a premonition in the film of disaster to come, namely, the outbreak of the war which separates Mitzi and Nicki, the chief protagonists in it, just as the White Lady of *La Dame Blanche* (for which a detailed script exists, even if it was fated not to be filmed—also by the outbreak of a war, the second World War, this time) was a premonition of the dismemberment of the far-flung and mighty Austro-Hungarian monarchy, heritor of the Holy Roman Empire.

Schiller put it aptly in his

Alles wiederholt sich nur im Leben,
ewige jung ist nur die Phantasie;
Was sich nie und nirgends hat begeben,
das allein veraltet nie.

(*Everything in life's repeated,*
Ever young is fantasy;
Only that which never happened
Falls not in antiquity.)

The origin of the White Lady is lost in the mists of time, indeed as far back as many centuries ago, if we are to trace one of the legends that surround it, namely, the rock on which the Castle of Duino on the Adriatic above Trieste is built. There are, in fact, two castles in the Trieste area, those at Miramare and Duino. The former was built by Franz Josef's younger brother, Maximilian, before he embarked for Mexico with his Belgian wife, Carlotta, and the latter by the Princes of Thurn und Taxis, an ancient Austrian family very close to the Hapsburgs. (Trieste and the whole area there were Austrian then.) Now, when seen from the sea, the rock on which the castle of Duino is built has the shape of "a white lady" (white, because the rock is white, and, with a little imagination one can make out the shape of a lady.) At any rate, the villagers around the castle think that the legend of the White Lady is somehow connected with the

Castle Duino. They have even named a local restaurant (famous for its seafood, incidentally) La Dama Bianca (Trieste and the area having, of course, long since been ceded to Italy). At the beginning of the century the Austrian poet Rilke was the guest of the Thurn und Taxis family in the castle. It was there that he wrote his *Duino Elegies.*

This is just one legend. *The Wedding March* and its milieu and the roots of that milieu in the thousand-year-old Hapsburg dynasty are full of stories, fantasies that, as you see, have lived beyond their sources, as fantasies have a way of doing.

Which emboldens me to relate the central idea of a film fantasy of Vienna once envisioned by the Viennese Fritz Lang (only three of the directors of the fifteen notable "Vienna films" I named were themselves Viennese—Stroheim, Sternberg and Willy Forst) told me by him during a night of autumnal reminiscence, a film he dreamed fondly of making in 1933 but which violent political events prevented, built around an idea of the purest and most endearing fantasy, to have been called *Die Legende vom letzten Wiener Fiaker* (The Legend of Vienna's Last Hansom Cab) and to have been filmed entirely in Vienna. It was to have been an idyll of the Hauptallee, one of the fashionable thoroughfares, where automobiles were not permitted, only graceful horse-drawn carriages. With the fall of the Hapsburg dynasty comes a sweeping away of the old order and old decrees, autos are now permitted on the Hauptallee. But this is too much for one of the old coachmen. Brokenhearted at the change in the city, he dies and, having been a good and faithful coachman, with long years of service, he goes to Heaven—with his two horses and carriage, naturally. He has no intention of being separated from them. But St. Peter stops him at the gate. "You can't bring that in here," he says.

"The hell I can't!" says the coachman. "If I can't take my horses, I won't go in."

Then God is called to arbitrate the matter and says, "They are very nice horses, but I can't break the rules. It's decreed that horses go to their own Heaven."

"So," says the coachman, "you've got decrees here, too?" Then he makes so eloquent a plea for his horses, who served him in life so well, that God relents and with a smile says, "Very well, then, you will be my own coachman—you will drive me." God gets in the carriage, the coachman puts his old top hat back on at a rakish angle, jumps up on the driver's seat and joyously tugs at the reins as the coachman and his horses enter Heaven and the wheels of the cab dissolve into the stars of the Great Dipper, which is God's own great carriage. . . .

Does this surprise you as being from the director of *M?*

The Nazi hydrophobia having forced Lang into exile, he made the fantasy that was dancing in his head in Paris, where he met a colleague refugee—the fabulous Ufa producer and mentor of so many ace German directors before Hitler—Erich Pommer. Together they made a fantasy set in a carnival in Budapest about a likable ne'er-do-well who goes to Heaven much before his time and is given a chance to redeem himself on Earth again. As you have guessed, the film was *Liliom,* from the Molnár play. If it was not *Die Legende vom letzten Wiener Fiaker,* it was at least a memorial to it, and this evocation of it is in memory of it too.

But Ophuls, for all his brilliance, for all his virtuosity (and he was one of the very greatest cinema virtuosos), marinated the stories he adapted from Schnitzler and Zweig in sentimentality. The originals of *Liebelei* and *Letter from an Unknown Woman* are merciless. *The Wedding March* (like *Foolish Wives* before it) does not soften the hard-lipped rue of the story but tells it with ruthless logic and psychological realism that always is at the core of truth no matter how contemptuous of the box office that truth might have been. It is not that Ophuls compromised for the box office's sake (*La Ronde* is nowhere as brutal as *Reigen* is) but he sought and found other values, just as valid, in his sources, ranging from the heady visual cocktails of *Lola Montes* (which is really so much more than that) and *Le Plaisir* (after three stories of de Maupassant, winningly if less sardonically told than their originals) to the exquisite *Kammerspiel* (chamber music) things like *Liebelei* and *Letter from an Unknown Woman.* What a pity that he never tried his hand at putting on the screen Schnitzler's *Anatol,* whose seven witty dialogues match the ten acid ones of *Reigen,* and in which, encom-

passing the then new Freudian psychology, it is shown that sometimes illusion is more desirable than truth. *Anatol* is less recalcitrant for an adaptation than *Reigen,* though if you ever saw the De Mille version you'd never think so. But an Ophuls *Anatol* or a Stroheim *Anatol*—what missed opportunities! I use the plural because ideally we should have been vouchsafed them both. And why not the marvelous *Casanova's Homecoming* of Schnitzler, in which the aged seducer returns to Venice and tries a "last fling" only to find that the old life is done, irrevocably done, a bitter thing for so active a fellow to contemplate? And *Schweik,* too, with its irrepressible humor and fantasy of the man in the street confronting the establishment, its irreverence for all forms of authority, and a distrust for high-sounding words and attitudes. Is this asking too much? Well, then, it is asking too much. The history of all art is a constant succession of artists who have tried and often succeeded in "asking too much." *Anatol,* after all, is Schnitzler's "Viennese" quintessence of amorous frivolity tinged with his irony—and Schweik is Hašek's universal bumbling antihero, drafted into the Imperial Austrian Army, who becomes a sounding board for the author's withering satire against militarism and officialdom in all ages and all climes. Schweik's deadpan "There must be a higher reason" as his rationale of a bureaucracy he cannot understand is surely one of the world's great consolations, and he has become a divine innocent as endearing and as immortal as Don Quixote.

Before leaving our "School of Vienna"

films and filmmakers, I would like to recall an even earlier use of fantasy by Stroheim as far back as 1923–24 in *Greed*; Zerkow's nightmare dreams of digging up the crazy Maria Macapa's nonexistent gold dishes from a grave in a Caligaresque cemetery at night and Trina's nightmare dream that the disemboweled Maria, finally knifed by the exasperated Zerkow when she cannot deliver the gold plate, is haunting and taunting her with "Wanna buy a lottery ticket?" which had originally set into reaction the awful chain of woe that followed. Not forgetting the stylized insertions of long, bony arms ending in hands voluptuously fondling gold and gold things and pouring cascades of golden foam from leather-bound treasure chests . . . Here Stroheim carried realism so far as to go beyond realism into surrealism, though *sans* the irrational, non-contextual arrangement of the material characteristic of the surrealists. He used his grotesque images as metaphors, as symbols, "so close to the reality itself," as I wrote in my foreword to *The Complete 'Greed,'* "that they could almost pass for it." In *Greed, The Wedding March* and *Queen Kelly*, which followed, the line of demarcation between reality and exaggeration was erased and replaced with metamorphoses which took place before your eyes.

And apropos Stroheim as director of a film of *Schweik,* let me recall Rudolf Arnheim's 1940 dictum: "In my opinion there are two men able to make a great film on Hitler and fascism. One of them is Erich von Stroheim, whose film probably will never be made because it would push the cruel truth too far beyond any-thing a film producer would accept. The other man is Chaplin." Of course, Chaplin made his, *The Great Dictator*. Stroheim, it is true, never made his, but as far back as 1921 he delivered a blast at the atrocity of war in the famous episode in *Foolish Wives* of the "rude" American marine who doesn't pick up the lady's dropped bag because he has no arms. And he followed that with a script for *Merry Go Round* in which his glints of the havoc of war have the terrible indictment of those in Pudovkin's *End of St. Petersburg*. This wasn't made, either; at least it wasn't made as he would have made it had he been permitted. In *The Wedding March* and *La Dame Blanche* he could only brush against the war as a terrible imminent thing. (As the populace in front of St. Stephen's Cathedral, in the former, cheers the Austrian soldiers leaving for the Eastern Front, Stroheim superimposes over the departing troops the Four Horsemen of the Apocalypse from Revelation—they, too, are going to the Eastern Front, where the Russians await the garlanded Austrians, leaving in their wake the miseries of War, Famine, Pestilence, Death. This, too, was never filmed. As you see, Arnheim was right. They never have let Stroheim do more than touch on the subject of war. A script he did on air raid shelter life in Paris in the second World War, *Abri–50 Personnes,* also remained unfilmed.

We have spoken of sources, of literary works that were compromised in the filming either through box office necessity or the seeking after different values, but literary works were frequently also surpassed in the filming. Obscure plays like *Only a Dream* by Lothar Schmidt and *The Honest Finder* by László Aladar miraculously became *The Marriage Circle* and *Trouble in Paradise,* through the witchery of Lubitsch and his adaptors, Paul Bern and Samson Raphaelson. Similarly obscure novels, such as *Amy Jolly* by Benno Vigny and *Professor Unrat* by Heinrich Mann, were transmuted miraculously into *Morocco* and *The Blue Angel* by Sternberg. Stroheim accomplished the same feat by taking the preposterous libretto of *The Merry Widow* by Victor Leon and Leo Stein and, together with Benjamin Glazer, turning a banal operetta plot into a witty and sardonic satire on Central European royalty in that blithe period between La Belle Epoque and those fateful August days of 1914. Franz Lehár said of the film that if he had not already written the score, the motion picture would have inspired him to do so. And "Had I been more mature when I wrote it [*Professor Unrat*]," said Heinrich Mann, "I would have developed the character of Professor Rat more humanly, as in the film [*The Blue Angel*]." So, sources aren't necessarily sacrosanct, though, of course, sometimes they are.

But all this has just been a stage setting, sketches for the décor, to set the ambience against which the story of the making and unmaking of *The Wedding March* will be told. Films don't exist in a vacuum, though, alas, they would often like to make us think so. The real ones exist in the real world with all that it implies. "Things [read: values] do not cease to exist," said Paul Claudel, "because we leave them behind." It was perhaps the

chief strength of Stroheim as a director that he did not leave the human condition behind when he embarked on the making of a film. Not "The Human Condition According to L. B. Mayer's or Adolph Zukor's Hollywood," nor "According to Sovkino of Moscow" nor to the taste of "Mrs. Ufa," Ilya Ehrenburg's contemptuous reference to what the biggest film studio in Europe did to his *The Love of Jeanne Ney,* nor to the trumpery of so many heroes and heroines of fiction, or the gilded coxcombs and taffy harlots of the movies, but the human condition that is everyone's in the real world each inhabits at night in his dreams, which is his, and his alone, of all the people on earth.

"*The Wedding March* Story" begins, as does "The Hapsburg Dynasty Story," in which it is rooted, as a ghost story.

The roots go back to the eleventh century — 1020, to be exact — when a Count Radbot, one of the heirs to the original progenitors of the Hapsburgs (or Habsburgs), built himself a castle in northwestern Switzerland at the confluence of the rivers Reuss and Aare, a four-storey square tower, which seemed to attract hawks, of which there were a large number in the area. "The Count took this as a good omen," reports Hans Holzer, the Austrian parapsychologist in his *The Hapsburg Curse:** "True, they were not as glamorous as eagles, always considered as symbols of royalty or at least extreme nobility, but the mighty hawk . . . was a good hunter and fierce defender of his

*Doubleday & Co., 1973.

own. Thus the hawk was just as suitable for the symbolic representation of family honor as the more elevated eagle. Whether by accident or design, the fortress soon became known as the Hawk Castle, in old German, *havichsburg.* . . .'' By 1108, Count Otto, grandson of Radbot, was designated as Count of Habsburg.

There are two legends about this castle, which still exists, a picturesque ruin, in the canton of Aargau between Basel and Zürich. One holds that ''. . . a man once lived there,'' again quoting Professor Holzer, ''who was kind to the hawks that inhabited the grounds. But one day he did something terribly wrong, and the people of the land put a curse on him. Even his friends, the faithful hawks, left him. According to the story, he and all his descendants must suffer from the curse until the last one dies.''

The other has it that ''one of the counts became attracted to a beauty in the village'' below the castle hill. ''In the abrupt manner of the times,'' reports Holzer, ''a love affair followed, or perhaps he raped her, or perhaps a little of both. In time, the girl became pregnant. This was the more deplorable as she had been engaged to be married to a nice young man in the village before the roving eye of the count had fallen on her. The village swain wanted nothing further to do with her, of course, since it seems this was still before the age of chivalry. Disowned also by her own family, she had no place to go but up to the castle to confront her seducer. . . . [But] the count wanted nothing to do with her, too. She probably became hysterical, and he had her

thrown into the dungeon. At this point . . . the distraught girl may have uttered a curse against Count Habsburg and his family, taking the hawks in the yard as her witnesses. As long as there is a Hapsburg left alive, there will be birds around the castle, but when the curse has finally found its mark, the birds will leave as a sign that it is all over. . . . The story goes on to say that the girl died in childbirth and was buried with her baby on the grounds.''

There is even a third legend, which connects, concludes Professor Holzer. ''One of the young counts was killed in a hunting accident. An arrow meant for a stag hit him instead. The next day his body was brought back from the woods and the commotion allegedly aroused the villagers to run out of their houses to see what had happened. The mother of a girl who had been wronged by one of the men at the castle was among those who ran to look, but as she opened her door she almost fell over the body of a large bird. It was a hawk lying dead at her doorstep.''

Mitzi in *The Wedding March*, though affianced to Schani, is seduced during a brief love affair with Prince Nicki. Schani, too, is at first outraged and in Part Two Mitzi, too, is disowned by her mother for not marrying Schani. Up to this point, there is a parallel with the second of these legends. And since war breaks out that separates the lovers in the film, we leave them, not knowing what will become of them. Maybe Nicki will never come back. The director's pessimism is just as truculent here as it was in *Greed*. Not only are the demands of family insuperable, dividing the lovers, but that ultimate Great Divider, in the guise of war, divides the lovers too. They never had a chance. Thus does Stroheim show his scorn for the contrariness of life. Maybe *The Wedding March,* as a completely realized work of the director, never had a chance, either.

It began, he told me, when he and Harry Carr, ex-war correspondent and his collaborator on the script, decided to write it in seclusion, choosing a rented chalet high in the San Jacinto Mountains, sixty miles from Los Angeles, completing it at La Jolla, then a seaside village fourteen miles north of San Diego. Accompanied by an assistant and a secretary, Stroheim and Carr motored to the mountain villa, each occupying a separate bedroom for the first night. "I say 'first night,'" said Stroheim, "although there was no second night—not at first." What happened was that in the middle of the night (at 4 A.M., as it turned out), "I felt overcome by an incredible horror. . . . I don't mean there was a ghost in the room, chains rattling, or anything spectacular, just 'waves,' but simply terrifying 'waves,' and while I was trying to snap out of it, an organ started playing. . . . Well, what shall I tell you? By this time it was dawn. My secretary, who felt and heard what I did, and I both ran to Harry Carr's room but he'd gone, he and my assistant, driving off in the car, presumably back to Los Angeles.

"'You don't think it could have been the wind moaning in the organ pipes?' asked my secretary plaintively.

"'What wind?' I said. 'All the windows were closed.'

"'Maybe a draft . . . ,' he ventured, even more plaintively.

"'Sure, a draft,' I said, 'a draft playing Bach!'

"That morning we hitched a ride back to Los Angeles ourselves and confronted Carr, abashed but quite candidly admitting that, not knowing what to make of it (he heard and felt what we did, too), he decided to get the hell out of that place. That afternoon I went to the renting agent and told him what had happened. He smiled sadly, saying, 'I'm not surprised you're back but I was hoping that the jinx on that house was broken by now. . . .' And he told this story. . . ." Stroheim took a swig from his pocket flask and continued.

"The house had been built for his own use by an architect who had won first prize at the Chicago Exposition and who, though his total fortune amounted to $150,000, spent $250,000 on the house—a sort of 'Erich von Stroheim Production,' if I may put it that way. . . . A hundred thousand dollars' worth of debts and not a cent to live on. After a terrible mental struggle with himself, fighting the anguish for which he saw no remedy, he shot himself in his room . . . the 'master bedroom,' if you please . . . *my* room . . . at four o'clock in the morning one night. . . .

"His wife—did I forget to say he had a wife? —grieving over her dead husband—slit her throat in the same room. Don't ask me why she chose four in the morning to do it, too. Ask the coroner, he had it all figured out. I suppose each of them, during the awful hours of spiritual torture, then of physical torture, forever charged the atmosphere of that room with waves of terror and that, as long as the spell had not been broken, each time the clock struck four in the morning, like tuning in on a specific wavelength, a flow of fear, the same dread they must have felt, suddenly flooded this room. Maybe, before dying, one or both of them had turned on the electric organ (which we later found in the house, locked, of course, and full of cobwebs), a magnificent electric organ, like they used to have in the big movie palaces in the silent days, one of the expensive follies among the installations there, the one they probably expected would bring them the most joy. . . .''

The renting agent, reported Stroheim, concluded by saying that whoever rented the house always came back with the same story, and he offered to refund their rent, which Stroheim refused. ''If that's all it is,'' he said, ''it'll be all right. I like the idea of writing the story of *The Wedding March* in a place like that. It's going to suit it . . . in a way, *The Wedding March* is a ghost story, too.'' And then he recollected that when he was filming *Greed* three years before in San Francisco, he sought out the very house where the actual murder took place that was the impetus for Frank Norris's novel, *McTeague*, on which *Greed* was based, so that the actors would become ''permeated'' with the fear and dread of that unhappy house.

Then the five, with the renting agent as host, celebrated with a fine lunch, and the four drove back to the mountains that evening. ''The second night,'' said Stroheim, ''was as

quiet as an empty cathedral.'' Then, ''Like those lines. . . .

Still wie die Nacht
Tief wie das Meer . . .''

''*Soll deine Liebe sein!*''* I finished. He smiled. ''That's it, that's the way it was from then on, for the next several weeks, during which Harry Carr and I wrote *The Wedding March.''*

Does the gentle reader wonder what credence one can place in this? Hark then to this from Rebecca West in *Recollections of Virginia Woolf by Her Contemporaries:* ''Once Virginia wrote me a delightful letter, and I had it framed and hung it on the wall of my room, with one from D. H. Lawrence on one side and one from George Moore on the other. Suddenly I looked up at the wall and Virginia's writing had disappeared. There was just an oblong of paper in the frame. Two days later I read in the paper that she was dead. . . .''†

What was the milieu of *The Wedding March*? Though teetering on the edge of what was to be the first World War, life in the ''upper world'' of Vienna went blithely on, just as it did in the ''upper worlds'' of England of the Windsors, Germany of the Hohenzollerns, Italy of the Savoys, Spain of the Bourbons, France of M. Poincaré, and Russia of the Romanovs. In the United States, Mrs. Vanderbilt and President Wilson held sway. Four

*Still as the night
 Deep as the sea,
  So should your love always be.*
†Edited by John Russell Noble (William Morrow, 1973).

years earlier, Halley's comet had streaked across the sky and would not pass again for seventy-eight years.

Comets are traditionally associated with disasters. The first one recorded (by the Chinese in 240 B.C.) was supposed to have presaged the destruction of the Temple of Solomon in Jerusalem in A.D. 70, and subsequently the Norman invasion of Britain in 1066, the death of King Philip Augustus of France in 1223, and the plague that swept Europe, the "Black Death," in the fourteenth century. Its appearance in 1910 was regarded as presaging still another catastrophe, the outbreak of the first World War in 1914. The legendary White Lady floating through the corridors of Schönbrunn and then out over the city of Vienna on the eve of the assassination at Sarajevo was to "consolidate" it. With two such "omens of disaster" against her, Austria hadn't a chance. We will return to the legend of the White Lady as it is reflected in von Stroheim's *La Dame Blanche,* never filmed.

"Viennese life on the surface was gay and feckless" is how Virginia Cowles described it in her vivid *1913: An End and a Beginning.* "No capital in Europe seemed to have the same intimate charm as Vienna, with its baroque buildings and leafy avenues, its agreeable inefficiency, its mixture of races, its strains of waltz music and its seven hundred street cafés, crowded with laughing, talking people, no matter what time of day. Whipped cream melting into black coffee seemed to reflect the capital's air of froth and impermanency. The Viennese were passionately attached to their city. The Ringstrasse, a broad street planted with four rows of trees in the manner of a Paris boulevard, and the Kai which ran along the Danube, were the glories of the capital with its succession of palaces, monuments and public buildings intermingled with parks and gardens. The Prater, a huge wooded common to the east of the town, was the playground for people from all walks of life.* The aristocrats took early-morning canters under the chestnut trees along the Kärntnerring with its fashionable boutiques, cafés, hotels, or drove their carriages along the Hauptallee,† and drank their morning coffee at Konstantinhügel and Krieau; while the lower classes flocked to the Wurstelprater, which was a permanent village fair with merry-go-rounds, Punch and Judy shows, moving pictures and sensational sideshows. But what gave Vienna its most distinctive charm was its environs. Ringed by mountains less than three hours away by rail, it offered its inhabitants hill resorts of majestic beauty, which were particularly popular in the summer months. Yet despite its outward appearance of friendly intimacy, Vienna was not a capital that many foreign diplomats enjoyed. It was a place to visit, they said, not to live. The truth was that Viennese society was so haughty and exclusive that it had turned itself into the most parochial society in Europe. It took its cue from the Court, which operated an archaic Spanish etiquette. Everything depended on

---

*It served Stroheim as the principal setting for his earlier *Merry Go Round.*

†The fashionable thoroughfare on which Fritz Lang's *Die Legende vom letzten Wiener Fiaker* began.

pedigree. No one could go to Court unless he possessed sixteen quarterings. It did not matter how brilliant or charming or rich a man, unless every one of his ancestors, on both sides of his family, was impeccably well-born for the required number of generations, the doors were irrevocably closed to him. 'An Austrian might be Shakespeare, Galileo, Nelson and Raphael in one person,' wrote the American Minister, 'but he would not be received in good society if he did not possess the sixteen quarterings of nobility which birth alone can give him.' . . . The whole nation lived in the traditions of the sixteenth century, when the proud Hapsburgs ruled the whole of Europe with the exception of France, England, Russia and the Scandinavian countries. . . . Although the Emperor Franz Josef cared nothing for society, and himself led a Spartan existence, he was a stickler for the haughty etiquette which stifled the Viennese Court. He would not allow a single rule to be relaxed, a single exception to be made. The etiquette was part of the Hapsburg tradition and he was the guardian of it. . . . Despite the strictness of Viennese society, the unmarried girls of the aristocracy [the *jeunesse dorée*] had a unique position. Whether Princesses or Duchesses they were all referred to as the *Comtessen*.* And the *Comtessen* had a much freer, more amusing life than unmarried girls anywhere else in Europe. In the first place, they were allowed to smoke. After every dinner party the guests, ladies included, always retired to a smoking room: 'One's aesthetic sense is rather

shocked,' wrote Lady Paget, 'by seeing a beautiful young woman with bare shoulders and a blazing tiara, lighting a big cigar over a lamp . . . and there are evening parties with nothing but *Comtessen* where the fumes of havanas have been seen hovering in the air. . . .'* Whereas the *Comtessen* boasted many pretty girls, few foreigners found the male members of the Austrian aristocracy either attractive or interesting. Interbreeding had weakened their physiques and not quickened their brains. They seemed to have the same profiles, the same mannerisms, even the same gait—they walked with long strides, heads bowed forward and shoulders slightly bent like the Emperor's. Cut off by snobbishness from intellectual stimulus, they had few aims or interests apart from the pursuit of pleasure. They had three passions: shooting, gambling and women. Shooting came first and took up eight months of the year. It began with the chamois in August, followed by stag and roe-deer,† the partridge and the pheasant. Then came the wild boar season, and in February, amongst the mountains of snow, the arduous shooting of the hinds.‡ When this was over the stalking of the capercailzies began. There was no lack of terrain to shoot over for almost all the noble families of Austria and Hungary were immensely rich, owning much land.§ Prince Liechtenstein kept over one thousand one hundred gamekeepers in Bohemia alone,

*Prince Nicki's mother smokes cigars in *The Wedding March*.
†Reflected in Part Two of *The Wedding March* and in *La Dame Blanche*.
‡Reflected in Part Two of *The Wedding March*.
§Except when they fell upon hard times like the Wildeliebe-Rauffenburgs in *The Wedding March*.

*The Countesses.

and drew a rent roll in Moravia said to have exceeded one hundred thousand. In the same province, Prince Schwarzenberg had vast interests including ninety-five castles; and in Galicia the Potocki estate exceeded half a million acres. Among the great Hungarian landowners were Prince Esterhazy, Marquis Pallavicini, the Karolyis, the Andrássys and the Zichys. The only time the male members of the aristocracy were certain to be in Vienna was from the beginning of April to the end of June,* when the gambling season was at its height and the racing was on. . . . If it was fashionable to race and gamble, it was even more fashionable to have a mistress; two or three mistresses if possible. The titled youth usually formed liaisons with actresses and dancers. It was a recognized custom that stars of the first rank should have noble lovers and some of them were protected by a curious agency. The *corps de ballet* of the Hofoper, for example, was organized into a league, known as the *Tugenbund,* 'the League of Virtue.' This association systematized the relations between the dancers and their aristocratic lovers. When a cavalier selected a mistress, the association stipulated a contract in her behalf which established beforehand the indemnity which he must pay her, as having been well served, when he took a wife or left her.''

Like the Emperor, they showed little or no interest in the arts or sciences—that was left to the Jews of Vienna—Freud, Herzl, Mahler, Oscar Straus, Schoenberg, Schnitzler, Hugo von Hofmannsthal, Stefan Zweig, Martin Buber, Karl Kraus, Max Reinhardt, Kafka and their like—but these were as much citizens of the world as citizens of Vienna. It was not, as Miss Cowles points out, that Vienna was growing as a literary and artistic center (not to mention as the fountainhead of psychoanalysis through Freud, whose probings into the deepest recesses of the human psyche were termed *Jüdische Schmutzmedizin* [Jewish smut medicine] by his ''Aryan'' colleagues) but that these writers, poets and musicians were fertilizing other capitals of the world with their talent, too, while in the case of Freud, that supreme doctor of the soul, who revolutionized the way men think, his fertilization went beyond psychiatry into almost all spheres of human thought, while in Berlin his co-religionist, Paul Ehrlich, revolutionized medicine as a healing art to a degree just as far-reaching.

And so, though male aristocracy was never seen in the literary cafés like the Griensteidl, they *were* seen at the Jockey Club, Madame Sacher's (whose place got to be known as the ''Hotel Hapsburg'' for the heavy royal traffic in its *chambres séparées*) and whose cigars were as famous as her tortes, the Bristol, Demel's for midafternoon *Schale Gold,* coffee with *Schlagober,* and, of course, the Salle Barbosetti, the ''in'' rendezvous for officers and titled idlers in this chic center of fencing and pistol marksmanship.*

The one thing the aristocracy and the

*Exactly the period covered by The Wedding March and Prince Nicki's presence in Vienna.

*Luigi Barbosetti founded the code of dueling with rapier, saber and pistol. In Stroheim's Merry Widow, a title precedes the duel between the Princes Mirko and Danilo: ''According to the Code Barbosetti.''

bourgeoisie had in common was a blithe ignorance and a cosmic indifference to what made up the intellectual life of the capital.

And if the social caste system was a rigid one, the ritual of the Roman Catholic religion to which the Court adhered was just as rooted in tradition, just as inflexible.

It started with Constantine, first Christian emperor of Rome and founder of what was to become the Holy Roman Empire. In 1493 the Hapsburg Emperor Frederick III proclaimed his famous "A.E.I.O.U." dictum: *"Austria Est Imperare Orbi Universo"* (All the World Is Subject to Austria) which became the first motto of the House of Hapsburg.* And, indeed, by 1519 the Hapsburgs ruled over most of the then known Western world. This world hegemony was symbolized by the cross over the orb surmounting a crown flanked by two angels blowing their trumpets atop the roof of the State Chancellery building in the Hofburg Palace in Vienna to let the world know that Austria was the true defender of the Catholic faith in the world. The Emperors of Austria, throughout their long line of successions, were the only Roman Catholics who could veto the election of a Pope, so strong was the ecclesiastical power of the Hapsburgs and so intertwined was the Catholic Church with this ruling house. The old joke "more Catholic than the Pope" was no joke here. The Hapsburgs were. Did not one of the early Hapsburg emperors, Rudolph, son of Albert IV, when the imperial scepter could not be found during his coronation, seize the crucifix from the high

altar, flourish it aloft and cry out, "Here is the symbol that has delivered us and the entire world! Let it be my scepter on this occasion!"? Professor Holzer reports that "contemporary witnesses reported seeing a reddish cloud above the cathedral at Aix-la-Chapelle during the coronation ceremony. The cloud took on the shape of a cross, which led the witnesses to assume that Rudolph von Hapsburg was indeed the true successor to the first Christian Emperor, the Roman Constantine. But the cross which the Hapsburgs were yet to bear in the ensuing centuries might also be seen in the seemingly supernatural appearance of a cruciform cloud."

The Corpus Christi procession which is re-enacted in the film is of course the celebration of the Body of Christ which took place on the Thursday after Trinity Sunday in June* to commemorate the institution of the Eucharist. Partaking of the bread and wine at Communion, symbol of the Last Supper, is a sacrament which Catholics believe actually becomes the body and blood of Christ by transubstantiation. In many Catholic countries (the religious holiday is still celebrated in today's Democratic Republic of Austria) the day is marked by a great procession and with much show of flowers. (In Poland it used to be that no Jew was allowed to watch the Corpus Christi procession and if found was roughly handled.)

As for the "old boy" himself, his many subjects — and they were as varied as they were

*Another variant was "Austria Will Be the Ultimate (Last) Nation."

*The time element in *The Wedding March* is inconsistent with this, but as "poetic truth" it works, the "poetic truth" being more important than the so-called "real truth."

many—had pet (or derogatory) names for him. The dual empire (*K.u.K., Kaiserliche und Königliche*—Franz Josef being the Emperor of Austria and King of Hungary) was a mixture of Teutons and Slavs, embracing, besides the Austrians and Hungarians (which included Magyars of every stripe), Czechs, Croats, Serbs, Ruthenians, Slovaks, Slovenes, Italians, Muslims, Rumanians, the Poles of Galicia, and the gypsies of all these persuasions. "Der alter Prohoska," the Czechs called him, after the old royal family's Czech name. With allusion to the self-proclaimed fact that he never read a book (although the Empress Elizabeth, the beloved "Sissi" of the blithe days when he courted her, had a monument to Heine erected) and was seen throughout a reign of sixty-eight years (longer than Victoria's) only in a succession of military uniforms, it was said that he had "the soul of a sergeant," and that his empire was a "Völkergefängnis" (a prison of the people), a huge Bastille, whose eight major nationalities consisted of a double ruling class (Austria and Hungary) and six oppressed minorities which it exploited.

Came the ultimate ritual, as it came for all the Hapsburgs. . . .

Before the doors of St. Stephen's, the funeral cortège paused for permission to enter.

Three knocks were made on the door.

"Who is there?" intoned a voice from within.

"His Royal and Imperial Majesty, Franz Josef, Emperor of Austria, King of Bohemia, Apostolic King of Hungary and King of Jerusalem," was the reply.

"We don't know him," spoke the voice from within.

Again three knocks were made on the door.

"Who is there?" asked the voice from within.

"Franz Josef of Hapsburg," was the reply.

"We don't know him," again came the voice from within.

And again were three knocks made on the door.

And again, "Who is there?" asked the voice from within.

"A poor sinner," was the reply.

And slowly the doors opened. . . .

Toulouse-Lautrec (who would have gotten along famously with Stroheim) once illustrated the sheet-music of a popular song of the period, "Eros Vanné," whose words by Maurice Donnay went:

Très vieilles malgré leurs vingt années,
Usées blasées—
Car je suis né
Sur un lit de roses fanées
Je suis un Eros vanné.

which could be freely rendered as:

Old despite their twenty years,
Blasé and full of rue—
And since I was born
In a bed of withered roses,

I'm a worn-out Eros too.

The drawing shows the little god, Eros, with a bandaged head and on crutches, with one foot in a plaster cast. Behind him, two young women sit at a bar.

Stroheim, too, in his script for *The Wedding March*, describes the broken cupids (which he called "amorettes") on the escutcheon of "the crooked little house on the crooked little street," the screen title that introduces us to the bordello where Prince Nicki goes, as the officer caste, the aristocracy, and the well-heeled bourgeoisie, were wont to go, "when day was done," in this case, to Madame Rosa's, the biggest *pouf* in Vienna, who ran the most expensive bagnio in Europe at 69 (naturally) Kölnerhofgasse. Stroheim liked ironic contrasts. Thus, he places this rowdy sequence between two love scenes that Prince Nicki has with Mitzi. It was a time when this institution flourished as it hadn't since the "deer parks" of the French kings. The Sphinx and 32 Rue Blondel in Paris, the House of all Nations in Shanghai, run like a department store with different specialties on each floor, the Central Hotel on the Avenida Almeida Ribeiro in Macao on the Street of Happiness—the only 9-storey casino-brothel in the world . . . and Madame Rosa's in Vienna, which still lives briefly but full-blown in *The Wedding March*. But the point of all this is a detail, two details, two nuances in fact, in the way the *bordel* is introduced, via the "nursery rhyme" title, "In a crooked little house on a crooked little street," followed by an exterior night shot of the street in front of a darkened house on which a lone policeman passes and a little girl in a shawl wheels a baby carriage. . . . In this connection, hark to the description the Czech author, Ignat Herrmann, gives of the Fifth District, the ghetto, of Prague: "In many streets, house after house was a brothel. . . . Behind the heavy, huddled walls of the 5th District, what a fantastic mixture there was of riotous living and strict Jewish orthodoxy! Cheek by jowl with the haunts of vice and debauchery were the austere houses of believing Jews who locked their doors at nightfall, kept the Sabbath and observed the high festivals in traditional style."*

*Draussen am Mauer'l beim heurigen Wein
Fühl' ich die Welt ist so weit, so weit. . . .*
— Oscar Straus
"Ein Walzertraum"†

That summer of 1914 seemed as if it would last forever. There was no reason for it not to, a long "golden afternoon," in truth, as the Edwardian era in England and La Belle Epoque in France were drawing to a close, and, like sunsets, never did the sun shine more resplendently, never was the glow it gave off, its *douceur de vie*, more radiant. And the Vienna of the Hapsburgs, "Alt Wien"—Old Vienna—was now as old as it was ever going to be.

*Quoted in *Kafka and Prague* by Johann Bauer, Praeger, 1971.
†*Over a glass of the heurigen wine,
Big seems the world to me, seen through the vine. . . .*

The cataclysm unleashed in August would have been unleashed even if the incident at Sarajevo had never taken place. The army had been yearning for it and was now coming to the end of its patience. One pretext was as good as another. How could they lose against a little pipsqueak nation like Serbia? And her ally, Russia? Who could take Russia, militarily, seriously? They lost as much as they could lose —everything.

For once the Austrian imperial policy of aggrandizement by royal marriages with other nations instead of by wars of conquest was bypassed. Perhaps it was because the summer had lasted too long and by August everyone was bored. The Wildeliebe-Rauffenburg family in *The Wedding March* worked out its own policy of aggrandizement, though a bit late in the day, through a fortuitous (albeit love-less) marriage, the war ending it all for them, too, as it did for Austria. In a cataclysm the only survivors are the profiteers, those who batten on cataclysms, and Vienna had them too. Even the huge bell, the "Pummerin" in the north tower (*der alte Steffl*, as it was affectionately called) of the Stefanskirche was stilled. Vienna lay prostrate.

Stroheim ended his *Merry Go Round* with Vienna a ruin and the Prater trying pitifully to stir itself into life again. And once more, in *The Wedding March*, does he echo those parlous August days that were to herald the crucible of fire that awaited the once lovely city — *Kaiserschmarren*, brothels, Schönbrunn, ghettos and all. . . .

In 1913 in the district of Holstenwall near the Reeperbahn in Hamburg there occurred a bizarre murder reported by a Czech journalist, Hans Janowitz.

In 1915 began the death struggle of Verdun that was to last into 1916.

In 1916, Franz Josef died, and two years later a collapsed Austria begged the Allies for peace.

And in 1919, that Czech journalist, Hans Janowitz, wrote a film with Carl Mayer inspired (if that's the word for it) by the Holstenwall murder, titled *The Cabinet of Dr. Caligari*. Europe was ripe for such a film — but a zombie who carried out his master's orders (in the case of Caligari, to kill) was old stuff. Some three hundred years before, at the Hapsburg Court of Rudolph II, one of the favorites of the Emperor was Rabbi Löw, creator of the "Golem," which also did its master's bidding (but in the case of Rabbi Löw, to serve the deni-zens of the ghetto).

Speaking of Rudolph II, although insanity was to run intermittently through the Haps-burgs, it galloped where he was concerned. So unbalanced was he that his ministers had to delegate his imperial powers to his brother, Mathias, who succeeded him. He is remem-bered chiefly for his passionate interest in science, which brought the astronomers Kepler and Tycho Brahe to his court, not to mention his obsession with all manner of hokus-pokus which brought the cabalist Rabbi Löw and alchemists to his court, a veritable witches' cauldron of the black arts presided over by a monarch half-crazy with fear. His alchemists he locked up under orders to make gold in what came to be known as "The Little Houses on the Little Golden Lane." (Madame Rosa, keeper of the lupanar in "the crooked little house on the crooked little street" in *The Wedding March*, made gold there, too, through a different [and surer] kind of alchemy.)

But 1914—what a year it was! Isadora Duncan and Diaghilev and the Ballets Russes were the rage of Paris, as were Stravinsky, Prokofiev, the Groupe des Six in Paris and The Five in Moscow, not to mention what Schoenberg was doing to music in Vienna, making it sound as if written for the Chinese scale rather than like "Wien, Wien, nur Du allein!," Cubism was the chic thing and Klee, Franz Marc, Picasso, Modigliani, and Kokoschka, not forgetting Schiele and Klimt of Vienna, were among the painters of the moment. Art Nouveau was *the* thing and Wiener Werkstadt was turning out the most charming of *the* things, if we could have overlooked the frosted crystals of Lalique in Paris (as if anyone *could*). Josef Hofmann, Caruso, Ysaÿe, Kreisler, John McCormack, Paderewski and the young Heifetz were making concert audiences swoon in all the capitals (including Vienna) . . . and little Mitzi Schrammel, who couldn't care less about all this, happened to be standing next to Prince Nicki on his horse, both waiting for the Corpus Christi procession to come out of St. Stephen's, and, being flattered that he smiled at her, smiled back at him . . . a *coup de foudre,* if there ever was one.

But we are ahead of our story. "The Wedding March Story" goes back a long way, to the late spring of 1926 when, after the worldwide success of Stroheim's *The Merry Widow,* he was approached by a genial Irishman, P. A. (Pat) Powers, whose Celebrity Pictures Company produced Class "B" and, alas, even Class "C" films, but who made a fortune out of them. The two hit it off immediately, Powers having a good ear for tall stories and a taste for Scotch and Irish malt whiskies, both shared by Stroheim. They talked pictures and Powers said to him, "What would you like to do next?"

"I was just waiting for you to ask me that," said Stroheim, and he told him. It was the film for which his late-lamented and unfinished *Merry Go Round* had been the matrix, a film to be called *The Wedding March,* again about pre–World War I Vienna, again about a romance between an aristocrat and a girl of the people. A good picture could be made of the story for $300,000, Stroheim told Powers (*The Merry Widow* had cost only $247,000 and grossed $4,500,000). "Erich proposed that he direct it and appear in the leading role," reported Welford Beaton in *The Film Mercury* of September 1927. It was to take four months to make. "Pat told Erich to go ahead. Erich did. He began on June 2, 1926, and by the first of September had shot away $680,000 of Pat's perfectly good money—and as closely as he and Pat could figure it out, the picture was about half done. After two weeks of sad contemplation, they took a hitch in their britches and went at it again. By January 30, 1927, von Stroheim had slaughtered enough more dollars to bring the total casualties up to a million. *The Wedding March* is to be released in 8 or 9 reels. Von Stroheim's first cutting reveals the interesting fact that he had sixty reels of action—and that there still are a few more sequences he would like to take. My personal opinion is that the only way he can get money for more shooting is by killing Pat and taking up the matter with the executor of his will."

What brought the film to such an impasse?

Those thirty-six separate and distinct sets, for one thing, researched by Stroheim and his art-director, the ex–British Army captain, Richard Day, and built according to their specifications . . . Vienna, before the Great War of 1914, featured by its great central landmark, the thirteenth-century Cathedral of St. Stephen's, a replica of whose lower façade, interior nave and sunburst altar* against an elaborate grille were constructed to the last detail, with its steeples, belfries, cupolas and crosses soaring skyward, and the famous square, the Stefansplatz, before it. An inn, wine-garden, adjoining butcher shop and enclosed garden under the blossoming apple trees formed another elaborate set, duplicating in detail a *Heuriger* in rural Vienna on the banks of the Danube, where the young new wine was drunk, fresh from the surrounding vineyards.

Here were the old pump, the pig's trough, an arbor of vines and creepers and hidden bowers for lovers beyond which hedgerows bordered beds of marigold, jasmine and lilac, while over

*The sunburst altar was quite different from the actual altar of St. Stephen's but much more photogenic and dramatic than the actual one—another instance of Stroheim's "poetic truth" being more effective than the "real truth."

all, over all were enormous bouquets of apple trees in full flower, with entwined lovers' hearts carved on their trunks, from which a snowfall of pink and white blossoms fluttered down on the arriving guests like swarms of snowy night-moths, the street in front of the inn with its trolleys and beer carts clattering along and the clip-clop of horses' hooves. Interiors of magnificent proportions representing the halls, drawing rooms, boudoirs and galleries of the Viennese aristocracy were built in the Associated Studios, where the film was shot. (Not an inkling of the Prater, though, not this time—that was a "touchy subject" with the director, he'd been through all that before.) Several rooms of the Hofburg, where the Emperor resided, and in the summer palace, Schönbrunn, were duplicated. On Mount Alice, at a height of 12,000 feet in the Sierras, a *Jagdhütte* (hunting lodge) was built of the natural rock and timber found at the site, to represent mountain life on the Tyrol. Built also in the valley below was a baronial chateau, the family country seat of the Wildeliebe-Rauffenburgs, where Prince Nicki brings his bride for their honeymoon, complete with its trellised walls, ivy-covered gate, caretaker's lodge and all the rest. A convent, supposedly on the Austro-Serbian border, was also built, complete with medieval chapel, old stone corridors, nuns' cells, and terraced cloisters beyond which a rude wooden bridge had been thrown across a ravine over which cavalry were to pass on their way to the front, watched from the convent by a tearful Mitzi desperately looking for her Prince. . . .

Even the actual royal coach of the Emperor was borrowed from the Vienna State Museum along with its eight sets of gold-plated harness and the accompanying uniforms for footmen, postillions, outriders and attendants. And a real Vienna trolley was duplicated to the last detail, equipped to run under its own power along the tracks leading to an abutment to mark the end of the line in front of the inn. As for the Emperor himself, not only was he a dead ringer for old Franz Josef, but even his medals were correct, including (in their correct order) the Officers' Long Service Cross, the Court Jubilee Medal, Jubilee Cross of the Fourth Class, Order of St. George of Russia, his own medal turned with its face inward, the ribbon of Empress Maria Theresa, the Iron Crown of Leopold, the Medal of the Supreme Order of Austria-Hungary, St. Stephen's and First Apostolic King of Hungary, and the highest *K.u.K.* decoration of all, the Order of the Golden Fleece. For the Corpus Christi ceremonies, the Emperor's guard included meticulously uniformed Trabanten, Arcierean Hussars and Honved Lifeguards Mounted, the full panoply of Austro-Hungarian officer chic, resplendent in their uniforms of red, gold, black, blue and white. Leopard-skinned, plumed and cuirassed, the Radetzky Hussars were especially brilliant in their velvet dolmans, fur shakos and gleaming dress swords. The Austrian cavalry officers mounted on sleek black stallions, the Hungarian officers on gleaming white ones—the Austrian mounts' hooves painted a shiny black, the Hungarian mounts' hooves white, the Austrian helmets black-plumed, the Hungarian white-plumed. (By this time, Scriabin in Russia had already composed his twin piano sonatas, the "Black Mass" and the "White Mass." Stroheim's *The Merry Widow,* which had a seminude orchestra of whites in its orgy scene, was to have its counterpart, a seminude orchestra of blacks, in the orgy scene in *The Wedding March.*)

The procession from the cathedral, led by the full panoply of the Church's shamans, the Archbishop and ambassadors from the Holy See, followed by cardinals, Capuchin monks carrying candles and religious banners, the acolytes flanking them, finally the Host, the bread of the Eucharist, under the canopy, followed by the Emperor, Guardian of the Faith, and a long phalanx of officers.... All this was photographed in the then early two-process Technicolor, as much to contrast the luxurious display of the imperial and religious hierarchy with the drab plebeian populace as to exploit the dazzling spectrum of colors the scene offered.

And just as the director demanded thoroughbred horses for his cavalry mounts, he demanded blue-ribbon champion St. Bernard dogs and little leather casings for the feet of the hunting dogs to protect them against the crags and brambles for the mountain scenes of the second part. Just as he demanded (and got) a marriage license of the early years of the century for *Greed,* he demanded (and got) a real Viennese tabloid newspaper for Mitzi's father in the hospital room scene—the *Wochen-Ausgabe,* a well-known Austrian weekly of the period. Even the big box of chocolates that Prince Nicki brings Mitzi on his visit to the hospital room has the name of the swank *confiseur* from the fashionable Kärntnerring on it. Details, details . . . *"Le Bon Dieu est en le détail,"* said Cézanne, echoing Stendhal's "Truth is to be found only in details." . . . *En point,* a statue of the Virgin surmounts the gate to the entrance of the wine-garden, to the left of which is a fire-box and to the right of which is an advertisement reading, *"Sigi Ernst, Gummi Spezialitäten"* (Sigi Ernst, Rubber Specialties). Even the match-holders on the checkered tablecloths under the lanterns between the blossom-laden branches carry the inn's name, "Zum Alten Apfelbaum, Nussdorf" (At the Old Apple Tree, Nussdorf). Through Mitzi's bedroom window, when she comes to it in response to Nicki's whistle from the garden below, a chromo of a Madonna by Raphael is visible behind her and, on a chest of drawers to her left, what do you suppose is there? Think for a moment before I tell you. No other director would have remembered it . . . the box of chocolates Prince Nicki gave her in the hospital. Now, the Raphael and the chocolates are not visible in the film, only on the still photo of the scene. Many of the director's details are not visible in the film but the point is that he had to know they were there. Only in that way could he feel he had done everything he could do and it was up to the camera to catch as much of it as it could. Carlo Bisiach, a brilliant modern violin maker, when asked to exhibit one of his instruments, insisted on adjusting it first to "concert pitch," with the strings in perfect tune. When asked why he took that trouble since it was only a matter of exhibiting, not playing, the violin, he replied, "A violin is not just something to see, it is something to play on—it must be ready." I have a corollary anecdote about an esteemed colleague of Stroheim, the German director and one of the screen's supreme realists, G. W. Pabst. During the filming of *Pandora's Box,* after Wedekind, he asked Louise Brooks, as Lulu, just emerged from taking a shower and coming into the living room to greet her lover, Alva Schön (Franz Lederer), "What do you have on under that bathrobe?"

"My slip," answered Miss Brooks.

"Go back in the bathroom and take it off," said Pabst, which she did.

When she returned, wearing just the bathrobe, she smiled and asked her director, "Mr. Pabst, why did you make me take my slip off? The audience won't know that I have nothing on under my bathrobe."

"That's right," he replied. "The audience won't know, but *he'll* know," he said, pointing to Lederer, "and he'll play the love scene with you differently, knowing that, than he would if he didn't know it. And *that's* what I want, that *difference.*" Miss Brooks told me this story and I think it underlines the point I'm trying to make that the director must do everything he can think of to feel that the scene is ready to be played to the maximum that *he* can feel. If *he* feels it, the audience will feel it. Ergo—the director as psychologist.

Details are nuances, and good writing would

be inconceivable without nuances, sometimes of the most delicate kind, as in the anecdote of the young German girl visiting Paris who writes back to her friend in Berlin, *"Du, Liesl. . . . Bin sehr unglücklich weil ich bin in einer Franzosen verliebt und muss zu ihm 'Je vous aime' sagen wenn ich 'Ich liebe dich!' meine."* One could translate it and yet one can't translate it without losing it. Like what Granville Barker in his English rendering of *Anatol: A Sequence of Dialogues** meant in his prefatory note to Schnitzler's mercurial colloquies on the "grande passion": "It seems that in a faithful translation the peculiar charm of these dialogues will disappear," he said. "To recreate it exactly in English, one must be another Schnitzler, which is absurd. This is the only excuse I can offer for my paraphrase." And then he proceeds to transliterate "Ask No Questions," "A Christmas Present" and "A Farewell Supper" with such miraculous grace as to send one scurrying to the German original to see if it is, indeed, possible for him to have had so instinctive, so intuitive a feeling for the original, what the Viennese call *G'spür,* that in decanting the heady wine of Schnitzler's prose, in the process he did not spill a drop.

Before leaving *Anatol,* to which we seem to have been coming back, again and again, may we dream of what a film of it by Ophuls, let's say, would have been with the young Rex Harrison as Anatol and Roland Young as Max? Or, if it were done in its own language, then with the young Willy Forst as Anatol or Adolph

*Boston: Little, Brown & Co., 1917.

Wohlbruck (Anton Wallbrook to you). End of dream.

In *Foolish Wives,* lost among all the merry-makers, soldiers and sailors on leave, tourists, children and their nurses, is a blind French soldier, in the square before the casino of Monte Carlo, holding out a tin cup. Around his neck hangs a small placard that reads: *"Je perds mes yeux pour la France."* Detail, invisible in the film but visible on a still-photo of the scene.

In Stroheim's original script of *Merry Go Round,* a title precedes the scene where the old Emperor receives news of the assassination of the Archduke Ferdinand at Sarajevo: "If our inward griefs were seen written on our brow/ How many would be pitied who are envied now?" It is, of course, from the Italian poet, Metastasio, but who would have thought to find it here? Of course, no one ever saw the title. Detail.

In *Merry Go Round,* during a love scene between Franz (Norman Kerry) and Mitzi (Mary Philbin), a violin string breaks. Why? A nuance, the smallest possible, but a nuance, nonetheless.

("A distant sound is heard, as if from the sky, the sound of a string breaking, dying away, melancholy." [Chekhov: *The Cherry Orchard*])

Stroheim had a predilection for violins, as witness Franz playing one in *Merry Go Round,* the half-nude blindfolded "faun" on the bed playing one during Danilo's attempted seduction of Sally, Mitzi's father playing one in the wine-garden in *The Wedding March,* and

Prince Nicki playing the violin for Cecelia in Part Two of the film. This is interesting also because the Tyrolean violin maker, Jakob Stainer, second only to Stradivari and Guarneri as a maker of superb violins, was driven mad by the Roman Catholics of Germany and Austria, who resented his Lutheranism. In despair, he worked frantically against time, getting worse and worse, but producing his most beautiful violins. Today, there is a memorial to him in Absam, the Tyrol, his birthplace, and his violins are beyond price. Details.

During Mitzi's confession in St. Stephen's, in the background, a sacristan performs the ancient ritual of symbolically cleansing her of her sin by running a hot iron over a sheet of blotting paper placed on the melted wax candle drippings as she weeps her contrition through the grille of the confessional booth. "Pax tecum," says the priest through the grille. "Go in peace, my child." The sacristan lifts the blotting paper and the floor is immaculate again. Detail.

The final scene of Part One — Prince Nicki and Cecelia in their carriage, leaving St. Stephen's, after the wedding ceremony, after their confrontation with the tearful Mitzi on the sidewalk as they came out.

"Who was that sweet girl — in tears?" asks Cecelia in the carriage.

"I — I never saw her before," says Nicki.

But in the original script he said, "Probably one of those who go to other people's funerals and weddings to have a good cry." (Thus anticipating the character of Millie, the "mortophile," played by Zasu Pitts in Stroheim's *Walking Down Broadway* four years later.) Detail.

The script of Part Two begins with three omens of ill fortune: (1) the breakdown of the honeymoon carriage through a broken wheel; (2) a sudden downpour as the couple arrive at the family chateau (always a brooding and moody token in a Stroheim film); (3) Cecelia's tripping while crossing the threshold, final symbol of bad luck. This is reinforced by three old hags, among the retainers and villagers welcoming the honeymooners, like the three witches in *Macbeth,* foretelling the doom that awaits them. Details.

But the best detail of all is a scene that was shot for Part Two but cut from it, as so much else was cut. It comes right after the honeymoon night of Cecelia, abandoned by Nicki. Bitterly and in fury she tears her bridal nightgown to shreds. She now realizes what a loveless marriage truly means. And then it comes, a stylized interlude played against a velvet backdrop like a marionette insert to make a wry comment on the proceedings, to wit: "Against a velvet curtain with a crystal chandelier . . ." (I am quoting the script) ". . . with Schweisser in evening dress and Prince [Ottokar] in uniform — Schweisser looks around as if to divulge a great secret — he extracts two papers [checks] and hands them to the Prince — just then the Princess's (Nicki's mother's) head appears between folds of the curtain — she looks lynx-like, smiling in the direction of the two men — then she enters — slinks up to them from behind — looks at the checks in the hands of her husband — now they are both aware of her — smiling, she takes the checks from the Prince — looks at them devilishly — then, in that way of Maude George, wagging her head with raised cynical eyebrows, returns one check to her husband — folding the other and putting it into her stocking with great charm — revealing, the while, a perfect leg — The Prince is paralyzed — Schweisser laughs — she comes close to Schweisser and intimately puts her arms around him and kisses him as his reward, looking coquettishly over to her husband, who remains paralyzed."

Of course Nicki's mother puts Schweisser's half-million-kroner check in her stocking, just as prostitutes traditionally did. Didn't she sell her son to Schweisser as a titled husband for his commoner daughter just as surely as she sold herself? Which means she is aware of her exact role in this transaction and of the hypocrisy that passed for morality in old Vienna (and elsewhere) as a matter of the purest custom . . . marriages designed to create financial dynasties regardless of the personal fulfillment of the partners. Nicki's mother knows that. It doesn't stop her from doing it but she is aware of it. There is (or should we say was, although a still-photo of it exists and is reproduced in this book) a wonderful close-up of Nicki's mother *chez soi,* after the tragic death of Cecelia — mother, father and son, philosophically contemplating the future before a blazing hearth. Nicki's mother regards him with a look of mingled triumph at the coup she pulled (now that they've inherited Cecelia's magnificent dowry and Nicky is free to go back to his gay life as before) and

sympathy for her son, whose bitterness at his parents' callousness at Cecelia's death she can understand. She is not a monster nor is she a puppet, merely a human being, shall we say, an "all-too-human" (in the phrase of Nietzsche) being, with the wide latitude that this permits?

"Scutcheons that have lost their gilding," says Hofmannsthal in his description of rococo Vienna in the marvelous prelude to *Anatol.* And so has the escutcheon of the Wildeliebe-Rauffenburgs long since lost its gilding. "On a plaster-of-paris crest (Technicolored) with three hands pointing forefingers upward in a warning attitude, there is a crack straight through the crest, which is carried by little amourettes [Cupids] with bows and arrows on clouds, as pigeons coo and fly in and out." (Script)

Finally, Allan Janik and Stephen Toulmin in "Wittgenstein's Vienna" make the point that "in Old Vienna one could truly say that the bourgeoisie has torn away from the family its sentimental veil, and has reduced the family relation to mere money relation. For the would-be tycoon a 'good marriage' was essential." It was for the corn-plaster magnate, Schweisser.

The Wildeliebe-Rauffenburgs (that name reminds me that Eisenstein, a deep admirer of Stroheim, used to say that he couldn't always tell when he was in earnest and when he was kidding) as a ménage still have the trappings of luxury, when our story begins: a townhouse in Vienna, a villa in the Tyrol, both completely staffed, although the servants may not have been paid in some time, and a hunting lodge in the mountains. What they lack is hard cash and on that hangs the story.

Mitzi is the quintessence of the Viennese *süsse Mäderl,* or "sweet young girl," larding her words with a delicious dialect, full of romantic and superstitious notions, and harpist in the little music ensemble that plays nightly in the wine-garden in Nussdorf where she and her father work.

Schani is her boyfriend, a bruiser (as he would be, in case you had any ideas about Mitzi), professionally a butcher in the butcher shop attached to his father's wine-garden where Mitzi works. Quite conscious of his "he-man" good looks but just as numb to his low Viennese slang, *Pülcherdeutsch,* and vulgarity. He's been courting Mitzi for some time now and quite obviously hasn't yet managed to get to first base. The agitated state of his spleen when Prince Nicki catches Mitzi's eye is easy to understand. (Apropos, the young men of his class, the *Burschen,* to show their contempt of the upper classes, especially the military, used to shout a doggerel at them — and run — to the tune of the famous Radetzky March that started:

Ka' brot,
Ka' mehl,
Ka' rauchtabak!

This was Viennese cockney for:

No bread,
No flour,
No tobacco, too!

A favorite place for them to sing it was during the changing of the guard before one of the palaces — the Hofburg, Schönbrunn or Belvedere. Many of them may well *have* been hungry. . . .)

So, Vienna! The ancient municipium of Vindobona now become (according to the Austrian novelist Hermann Broch) "the metropolis of kitsch," "the city of operetta wisdom," the place of the "Happy Apocalypse." . . .

The most Eastern of European cities this side of Russia, it used to be said, starts in Vienna's Third District. During the four-power partition of Vienna following the second World War, the Russians simply consolidated their position.

The only city in the world where you can dial the musical tone "A" on the telephone — very right and proper, too, for the city of Haydn, Mozart, Beethoven and Schubert.

The only city in the world that has an "acoustic fountain" for the blind.

The only city in the world that could boast of a writer who could turn out two such utterly dissimilar works — the children's fantasy *Bambi: A Life in the Woods* and the adults' fantasy *The Diary of Josephine Mutzenbacher,* the pornographic classic — both by Felix Salten, according to that caustic critic, Karl Kraus, and others, who regarded the latter as Salten's best work.

The city Ben Hecht chose for a reminiscence of Madame La Sylph, ex-dancer ("the remains of a pirouette") now retired and running a ballet school in his *Specter of the Rose,* "I knew a vampire in Vienna once. She drank human blood to keep alive. They found her in a forest with a little boy. She had him in a sack." (Doubtless the notorious Countess Gisela von und zu Aschheim-Zondek.)

But also the city of the two most Viennese of composers—Johann Strauss and Oscar Straus. And it was Karl Kraus, the most Viennese of Viennese writers, polemicist and satirist par excellence, who made the fine distinction between them and Franz Lehár. He accused the composer of *The Merry Widow* of contributing to making Vienna "a proving ground for world destruction." Lehár was a cynical crowd-pleaser who wrote his operettas simply to make money, he said, and was consequently an enemy of all that was authentic in the city's contemporary culture. The success of Lehár's operettas was likewise in Kraus's eyes, a barometer of the moral degeneration of Viennese life. Lehár, he maintained, encouraged the forces of decadence by portraying it with such charm. Thus Lehár became the special object of Kraus's wrath because he was so good at carrying it through and popularizing this decadent art.*

*Such as the tenderness with which Johann Strauss sets to music the masculine-oriented:
    A fool is he who lets his chance pass him by,
    Unworthy of all that Love makes lovers sigh. . . .
from his *Thousand and One Nights* operetta, versus Lehár's cocky feminine-oriented "Silly, Silly Cavalier" song of Sonia in *The Merry Widow:*
    He that will not when he may,
    *When he wills it shall have nay. . . .***
**A footnote to a footnote is preposterous, but it might interest the reader to know that it was Lehár's setting of this text to music as a test that won for him the assignment to do the entire score for *The Merry Widow.*

For Kraus the true music of the *Volksseele,* the people's soul, were the Johann Strauss (and Oscar Straus) operettas and the folksongs, "The Old Refrain," *Paradise* (played by the "Vienna Swallows" ensemble in the wine-garden in *The Wedding March*), "Wien, Wien nur Du allein" (Vienna, Vienna, Only You!), "Im Prater blühn wieder die Bäume" (In the Prater bloom once more the trees), "Ich muss einmal wieder in Grinzing sein" (I must once more go out to Grinzing), and, of course, Schubert's "Was schöner kann sein als ein Wiener Lied?" (What lovelier can be than a Vienna song?)

And, of course, too, Richard Strauss's *Der Rosenkavalier,* composed four years before the story of *The Wedding March* begins.

The story of *The Wedding March* . . .

Let Freddy Buache, curator of the Cinémathèque Suisse in Lausanne tell it, as he does so lyrically in his monograph on von Stroheim:*

". . . Even if it doesn't correspond exactly to its creator's initial concept, this version [the released one] is a masterpiece like *Greed,* one of the greatest in the history of the silent film, alongside those of the screen's greatest— Chaplin, Griffith, Murnau, Eisenstein†. . . and among Pabst, Lang, Sternberg, Stiller, Sjøstrom, Keaton, Méliès, Pudovkin, Vidor.

"As for the second part, the producers ordered that it be composed of a two-reel sum-

*Freddy Buache, *Erich von Stroheim,* No. 71 in the Cinéma d'Aujourd'hui series. (Paris: Editions Seghers, 1972.)
†Note that Buache, too, includes Stroheim, Chaplin, Griffith and Eisenstein among the first four in the cinema hierarchy, and adds a fifth, Murnau, who would certainly be my fifth also.

mary of the first part, followed by the end of Nicki's, Mitzi's and Cecelia's story. . . . This version, titled *The Honeymoon*, infuriated Stroheim. He opposed its release and obtained that it be forbidden to be shown in the United States, but he was not able to prevent its distribution in Europe. In France it was released as *Mariage de Prince*.

"In *The Wedding March*, Stroheim takes up again, refines and gives added depth to his favorite themes, within the Austro-Hungarian monarchy. The seducer of *Blind Husbands*, the princes of *Merry Go Round* and of *The Merry Widow*, both of whom had been in love with lowly commoners, all are to be found in Nicki. And while this officer and nobleman may not be the cynical impostor of *Foolish Wives*, he has nevertheless retained the latter's demeanor, his taste for chambermaids, his sensuality and sense of humor, while the society in which he moves is no different from that which gathers around the gaming tables of the Monte Carlo casino. Behind the monarchial and ecclesiastical pomp are held both luxurious orgies and shabby working-class carouses, and despite the sumptuousness of the palaces it is impossible to forget men's misery or ferocity, or their tenderness and their need for love: neither the mud and the pigsty nor the apple blossoms and the moon haloing a crucifix. Between the terror imposed by the 'Iron Man' and the ever-present threat of the swelling Danube, between Law and Chaos, a mystery coalesces that sublimates flesh to the point of erotic ecstasy. That mystery is the one that transmutes Stroheim's astringent realism into radiant poetry, into a fraternal song of revolt and of the heart.

"Vienna, Anno Domini 1914 . . . shots of Vienna, the Cathedral of St. Stephen . . . the church interior . . . the Holy Virgin. . . . On a rooftop, the menacing statue of the 'Iron Man.' . . . Iris-in on the exterior of the palace of the Wildeliebe-Rauffenburgs.

"A luxurious bedroom: in her bed, the Princess Maria Immaculata,* mother of Prince Nicki, is wakened by her chambermaid. In the bed next to her, old Prince Ottokar is gingerly aroused from his sleep by his aide, whom he curtly dismisses and turns back on his pillow while his wife's pooch sniffs at his sheets. Ottokar sticks out his tongue at his spouse, who is particularly repulsive with her chin straps and face oiled with cold cream. They regard each other with cold fury and contempt. The Princess in exasperation throws a pillow at him. It is a typical morning, charged with sullen hatred.

"As for Prince Nicki, he is awakened by his own chambermaid who finds a woman's stocking among his clothes scattered in disorder about the rug. She shows it to Nicki. Seeking to kiss her, he pulls her down on the bed beside him, and takes her hand. The prince's breath makes the chambermaid wince. She leaves.

"Prince Ottokar is in the midst of getting into his uniform when Prince Nicki arrives and informs him of his financial problems. *Marry money,* says the father brusquely. *Or blow your brains out.* Prince Nicki says he'll ask

*Note that this cynical character is named after the Holy Virgin.

mama, and his father nods. In another room, Princess Maria is also getting dressed. She dismisses her maid when Nicki enters. Like with his father, he resumes his speech about his bleak financial situation. *Marry money,* she also says, and, after digging them out of the bottom of a purse handed her by her maid, she gives her son a few banknotes. Nicki kisses her in a gesture of affectionate complicity. She goes out (during which Nicki takes advantage of the opportunity to kiss the maid) and returns for him. They leave.

"This entire opening sequence is masterfully handled by the director through incisive images remarkable for their power to suggest the sarcasm and sordidness lurking under the frilly *décor,* oak and damask, velvet and satin, against which is played a comedy of manners in all its 'elegances'—played according to the rules of the game based on the reassuring complicity between master and servant.

"Bells. Church. White horses on the square. Officers in full regalia. A crowd presses forward to see the parade. Among the onlookers are Mitzi, her fiancé Schani the butcher, Mitzi's parents, and Schani's father. The procession goes by. The crowd cheers the imperial carriage. The soldiers present arms while Schani contemptuously spits. The Emperor descends from his coach. He is saluted by the Bishop. He enters the church with his entourage and kneels at the altar. The crowd stirs and tries to break through the police lines. The mounted guards try to maintain order. Mitzi looks up at Nicki in his dazzling uniform astride his sleek black mount. Nicki looks back at her. To get a better view, the whole family moves forward. Mitzi finds herself next to Nicki's horse. Nicki and Mitzi pursue their smiling dialogue of looks while Schani opens a picnic basket of provisions and proceeds to eat. An old woman offers Mitzi a bouquet of flowers and she hands it to Schani. He hands it back to the flower-seller with a disdainful expression, but when Nicki and Mitzi exchange smiles at his boorishness, he decides to buy it for Mitzi, after all. Mitzi smells the flowers' fragrance and, at Nicki's pantomimed suggestion, places some inside the top of Nicki's boot. He takes them, inhales them, places them under his tunic, and blows her a kiss. Bells. The celebrants inside the church kneel in their pews. Nicki's mother looks at Schweisser, the magnate, and his daughter, Cecelia, then whispers to her husband that she would be a good match for their son. *I've thought of it,* whispers Prince Ottokar, *but she limps, doesn't she?* To which Princess Maria smiles, *What's a little limp with twenty millions?* At the altar: Elevation of the Host. Bells. Trumpets. On the square the soldiers fire an honorary salvo. Up leaps a startled stallion and in coming down violently knocks against Mitzi who faints. She is carried to a doorway. A policeman telephones for an ambulance. The imperial procession comes out of the church. Bells. The crowd kneels at the passage of the canopied Corpus Christi. The guards salute. They go by, one after another, each time crossing the camera's field, while the procession's general direction is forward. The scene is directed with as great a precision as that of the guards themselves. Bells.

"At the hospital, Mitzi's father is at her bedside. She has twisted her ankle. The symbol is transparent: Cecelia has a limp. Mitzi is only temporarily immobilized by the sprain which resulted from the salvo (a phallic symbol): she fell following an erotic aggression. The foot, as in Jensen's *La Gradiva*, is a reference to sexual freedom. Nicki arrives in his handsome white coat. Mitzi smiles at him. He offers her a package. She asks his name.... *Nicki.... No, your last name.... Nicki ... It must be a mile long!* He kisses her hand. She opens the package. Chocolates. She is happy.

"Before the entrance of a wine-garden at night. Nicki, in uniform, dismounts from his fiacre, looks to the right and to the left, then enters the garden. A dog emerges from his rose-covered kennel and barks at him. A sow is nursing her sucklings. Nicki holds a kerchief to his nostril against the odor. He advances towards the tables under the apple blossom branches where the couples are sitting. Mitzi is playing a harp accompanying her father who is playing the violin. This scene could be ridiculous, but masterpieces always border on the ridiculous. Stroheim directs it with such disarming simplicity that it becomes irresistible, and projects only beauty. Mitzi's mother offers Nicki a table apart from the others: she doesn't want one of his rank to mix with the people. But he selects a table close to where Mitzi is playing. Mitzi notices him, smiles, raises her dress a bit to show him her still bandaged ankle. He drinks. End of

the selection. Applause. Mitzi, leaning on a crutch, is walking in the orchard with Nicki. They head towards an apple tree in blossom under which there is a crucifix. She kneels. He gives a military salute. They sit on a bench. He asks for a cigarette which is in the pocket of his coat. She gives it to him and lights it. He offers to thank her with a kiss. She refuses. They look towards the Danube. Mitzi says that sea nymphs sometimes emerge from the river and bring luck to whoever sees them; but that also sometimes the 'Iron Man,' whom she has never seen, carries off a sea nymph. Seeing him brings bad luck. Nicki kisses her hand. They head towards an abandoned carriage and sit down in it. Nicki has sat on a nail which he shows to Mitzi. They laugh. *You are made for love,* he tells her and kisses her. Mitzi's mother and Schani's father suddenly appear. Mitzi leaves. She realizes that she is still wearing Nicki's coat and hangs it on a gate. Her mother slaps her. Mitzi goes in. Nicki plucks some blossoms from a low branch, inhales them, then tosses them away. This love scene, one of the most beautiful in the history of the cinema to be set in a romantic key, is bathed in a paradisiacal light in which a veritable snowfall of silvery petals sparkle.

"Schani is out of prison. In his butcher shop, he threatens his men who are making fun of him. While he is chopping meat, Mitzi's mother informs him of her daughter's whereabouts. Schani takes a bite of raw meat, then, after crossing a puddle in which a swine is wallowing, nears the abandoned carriage. Mitzi is sitting in it, dreaming. He catches her unawares and kisses her on the mouth. Disgusted, she pushes him away. He threatens her. She hits him on the head with her crutch and hobbles quickly off. Schani, totally enraged, tears a twig of apple blossoms from a branch in a fit of impotent jealous fury (that one cannot see without thinking of Modot tearing at the pillows in *L'Age d'or*).

"Bordello. Black servants wearing music-hall armor (chastity belts with heart-shaped locks, gleaming hand and foot chains, pointed metal-studded *ceintures*) are opening bottles of champagne. Nicki is surrounded by women. In this house of pleasure he seeks to debase himself: deliberate self-abasement is the common choice for the icily dominating Stroheim personages, proving that the masochist is a narcissistic sadist. His father enters, notices him: they bow to each other. A throng of women pounce on the father. Nicki says he must leave to meet a nice girl. A goodnight kiss all around for his playmates in debauchery, and he leaves.

"The wine-garden. Out comes the dog, barking. Nicki gives him sausages to quiet him. He nears the house, looks up at the second floor window and whistles. Mitzi appears. She signals him not to make any noise, as Schani is sleeping next door (the butcher's striped jersey is hanging from a window next to hers). Suddenly she snatches with embarrassment at her underpants that had been hanging from the window on a line. She disappears inside where she quickly dresses. Nicki finds a ladder, climbs up, gazes at Mitzi, then tries to look past her into

the room at her bed. She turns his head away. He kisses her hand, then helps her descend.

"The remarkable stylistic characteristics of this sequence, which permeate the film as a whole, lie in the glistening conjunction of naturalism and dreams, of metaphoric prose and divinatory symbolism. At the first level of interpretation, the story appears to be composed of a somewhat affected idyll, but the coherence of its articulation clearly brings out its abundant resources. Schani's striped jersey suffices to circumscribe within the frame of the scene the menace he represents. The ladder that Nicki sets up in front of Mitzi's window expresses the expected sexual act. Mitzi, in snatching at her underpants, expresses assaulted modesty and draws attention to what, under her dress and in both their inclinations, will have to be won in order that the ritual of approach gives way to mutual possession. In the filigree of this romance, reality has been worked in, from the trivial to its catharsis.

"Bordello. Orgy. Corks pop. A Negro orchestra plays jazz. Schweisser, Cecelia's father, is talking to Nicki's father, who has collapsed on the floor because a corn on his foot hurts him. Amidst the heap of drunken officer-libertines and undressed women, he crawls. The orchestra plays at ever increasingly frenetic wailings.

"Nicki and Mitzi arrive under the tree. Now the river is swollen. A bird on a branch. They kiss. Nicki leads her to the carriage. On a branch, a startled owl. Clouds pass in front of the moon.

"Bordello. The orgy is taking on extravagant proportions. The two fathers, completely drunk now, are seated on the floor. Schweisser gives Prince Ottokar adhesive plaster for his corn. The Prince moistens the plaster by sprinkling champagne on it before Schweisser applies it to his little toe. They guzzle. The musicians laugh. Schweisser proposes to the Prince that his daughter, who has lots of money, marry the Prince's son, who has none. *How much? . . . Five hundred thousand crowns. . . . How much?? . . . A million!* stammers Schweisser. It's a deal. They drink to it.

"The moon seen through the clouds. Nicki brushes the petals and leaves that have fallen on Mitzi's knees. She is crying. He kisses her. The dog barks. They climb down from the carriage. *Will you always love me?* They kiss. The muddy waters of the raging Danube. The 'Iron Man' stalks off, carrying a sea nymph, superimposed over the turbulent river. Mitzi, frenzied, throws herself at the foot of the crucifix. Nicki tries to calm her and carries her back in his arms.

"Dawn. Schweisser returns home. Cecelia is at a window in her bedroom, fondling a dove. She comes forward, limping, to greet her father. He tells her of his talk with Nicki's father, and informs her of their agreement. *But I've never even seen the Prince,* she says. *You will, you will see him soon,* he answers. *How can I love him? . . . You have millions. Love will follow.* She weeps as she looks at her crippled foot. *A limping Princess!* Compassion floods over the father as he fiercely embraces his daughter and covers her face with kisses.

"Palace of the Wildeliebe-Rauffenburgs. Nicki's father and mother are trying to reconcile him to the *fait accompli. Love is one thing,* says his mother, sagely, *and marriage another.* Then turning, smiling sweetly, to her husband, *N'est-ce pas, Ottokar? . . . The wedding will take place the first of June,* the father peremptorily declares. *That's an order! . . . But she limps,* insists Nicki, *it seems to me on both legs! . . .* And his mother laughs.

"Church. Mitzi kneels, weeping, before the Blessed Virgin. Candles whose melted wax has dripped to the floor. A mother enters with her child. Mitzi goes towards the confessional. The verger gathers the fallen wax and glides a hot iron over a sheet of blotting paper covering the wax. Mitzi, seen through the grille of the confessional, is weeping. She is pregnant. *Peace be with you,* says the priest. The blotting paper has absorbed the wax. The floor is clean.

"The remarks that the seduction scene evoked here could now be repeated in connection with this sequence. There is no allegory, only a veristic style of direction which transcends itself because the descriptive narrative is tied in with obscure and deeply rooted emotions in the psyche of the director. The symbolism does not derive from a pre-established code, it is at the root of the story's veracity. In an atmosphere rendered unreal by the heavy silence and undersea-like nimbus of a place of worship, the everyday gesture acquires a diffuse meaning: the sperm-like wax running from the phallic candles which the verger makes disappear attests to Christianity's abhorrence of the carnal act and could serve to remind us of a line in Baudelaire's *Mon coeur mis à nu* (My Heart Laid Bare): 'Not being able to suppress love, the Church at least wanted to disinfect it—and invented marriage.'

"Cecelia in her room. She wears a simple white robe, like that of a nun. Before her, as she regards them, are her wedding gown and a head of Christ crowned with thorns. She looks at her wedding ring, her tiara, her crippled foot. Crown of thorns.

"It is raining. Schani is carrying a hog to the butcher shop for slaughter. Mitzi comes by. She tells him his father wants him. He shows her the newspaper account of the marriage of Nicki with the corn-plaster magnate's daughter to take place that afternoon at St. Stephen's. Mitzi cries. Schani assures her that he understands her tears. *The swine!* He pushes her, nevertheless, into a corner. She escapes his embrace and runs off. He catches up with her and forces his kisses on her. Disgusted, she spits them out. *I love him, she cries out, and I always will!* Schani's father, looking for him, arrives. He rescues Mitzi and slaps Schani. Schani threatens to kill Nicki. Schani's father consoles her, but Mitzi is afraid. . . .

"Bells. Church. Nicki and Cecelia exchange smiles. The choir sings. Now they exchange wedding rings. Cecelia has some difficulty getting the ring on Nicki's finger. He helps her. And now the fathers exchange smiles. End of ceremony. Bells. It is still raining. Mitzi has come to the church front. Inside the organist is playing *The Wedding March* but the hands that are playing are skeletal hands. This may refer to Schani's intentions towards Nicki but it also introduces into this game of sham happiness the matrix of that which no one there is thinking about, but which dominates the proceedings, the fact that bride and groom are walking down the aisle to a death march, she limping, he keeping pace with her.

"Apple blossoms of Cecelia's bouquet. Beaming faces of the parents. Nicki is helped with his cape. Schani has a gun in his pocket. Mitzi hugs his arm, to stop him. Schani, choleric, looks at Prince Nicki and Princess Cecelia coming out. The newlyweds stop for a moment before Schani and Mitzi. Nicki and Mitzi exchange an agonized look. The couple then get into their carriage. Schani lifts the weeping Mitzi onto his shoulder the better to see them departing. In the carriage, Cecelia asks, *Why was that girl crying? . . . I never saw her before, replies* Nicki. . . . *Won't the apple blossoms always remind you? asks* Cecelia. *Always,* answers Nicki. And the Iron Man laughs in the rain."

Mr. Buache has a problem with Part Two, *The Honeymoon* (or *Mariage de Prince,* as it was called in France). He sums up the balance of the film's plot, after noting that Part Two began with a summary of some twenty minutes of Part One: "Then we learn that Mitzi has kept her promise in order to neutralize Schani. She has agreed to marry him. . . ." But Mitzi, still in love with Nicki, faints at her wedding and this time Schani vows he will really kill Nicki. "While Cecelia and Nicki are honeymooning in their Tyrolean chateau, Schani follows them there and fires at Nicki. Cecelia, flinging herself between Schani and her husband, gets the bullet and dies. The murderer falls during his escape and is killed. Mitzi enters a convent.

"These tribulations do not in themselves mean very much, since Stroheim gives a palpable meaning to his anecdotes only through their visual impregnation or through their organization at the heart of the dramatic composition. Thus, in his novels,* his literary talents reside less in the fluidity of the text, the syntactical equilibrium, or the 'fruitiness' of his dialogue, than in the robustness of the structure, the relationships suggested between the situations, and the exposition of ambiguous elements through the play of counterpoint. As cineast, he possesses a remarkable sensitivity to photography and to screen space, but his mastery is greater still when it comes to the modulations of the narrative flow, both in a shot or in a sequence of shots. This is why, having been removed from control before the final cut, his films are but shadows of themselves: *Mariage de Prince* (The Honeymoon) is not more even than the shadow of a shadow. . . . That's why it's not enough to reconstruct

Paprika (The Macaulay Company, 1935); *Les Feux de St. Jean* (Paris: André Martel, 1954); *Poto Poto* (Paris: Editions de la Fontaine, 1956) (based on his 1933 scenario).

in a few lines the plots of Stroheim's works — it's necessary to restore their itinerary whose patterns, at all levels of interpretation, correspond to the principle of communicating vases* — where the real and the imaginary intermingle: the lily blossoms over the dunghill, the demarcation between the stage and the wings is blurred, the passion for truth exhausts itself only to be reborn in full delirium, and sovereign reason becomes folly's vassal."

It is the purpose of the "reconstruction" of Part Two via the still photos reproduced here to give this "palpable meaning" to Stroheim's narrative which Mr. Buache found lacking in the images themselves of the severely mutilated released version of *Mariage de Prince* (The Honeymoon) that he saw. I saw it, too, and know whereof he speaks. But how, you may ask, will still photographs accomplish what the film itself apparently could not? By the presentation of greater detail (wherein so much of Stroheim's meaning so often lay), by "the relationships suggested between the situations," of which he speaks, not to mention the showing of scenes not just cut down in the editing but scenes totally eliminated, scenes that are, indeed, as Mr. Buache points out, "at the heart of the dramatic composition" — at the very heart of the story's dramaturgy. For to Stroheim the play was the thing. It may not have been to Sternberg (I mean the Sternberg of his own films, not as the cutter of *The Wedding March*), to whom stories were only a "pretext" on which to construct a film, but it

*In chemistry there is a principle demonstrated by retorts connected to each other by a tube in which a liquid mass rises to the same level in each retort regardless of the shapes of the retorts.

was the *raison d'être* of a Stroheim film. It was what Lubitsch meant when he called Stroheim "the only novelist of the screen."* The technique to achieve this was only a means to an end, whereas for Sternberg technique was *the* end. If Jean-Luc Godard was right in his dictum that form was the outside of content and content the inside of form (and it certainly sounds right), it "explains" the form in which the Stroheim films appear as logically as it does the content contained within Sternberg's forms. At any rate, the reason Part One of *The Wedding March* "played" better even in its cut released version than Part Two is because there was proportionately less missing, which is to say, there was less detail missing. The unity of *The Wedding March* in its complete form, which it is the mission of the photographs in this book to reveal, was arrived at as a result of a thousand details in the service of a single concept. Leave any one out and you reduce the film by that much. Everything in a Stroheim film counts—there is none of what in music is called "passage work," no marking time until the next "big moment" through that often dubious procedure known as "development"—everything counts and adds to the cumulative effect that began with the first image. This must be understood to realize that the structure of a Stroheim film is the densest of any director's. Why must it be the densest? Why this fanatical zeal for detail? Look at the upper right-hand quarter of Manet's portrait of Zola with its Japanese print, reduced

copy of "Olympia" and other vignettes tacked on the wall, and the books and art catalogues in profuse disarray on the desk, and see how carefully these "inconsequential" details are painted, as if it were they who mattered rather than the subject, Zola. But by their verity they give the whole canvas a "cachet," a "tone"; indeed, the very signature of the painter. It is that way with Stroheim. Because every image is a signed image, the relationship between the images, their juxtaposition, is crucial to what he is trying to say, and cutting them out robs the film of nuances of motivation and the like. A painter says all he wants to say within the frame of his canvas but with a sensitive filmmaker like Stroheim, what the director wants to say resides in a succession of images within his "frames" and you cannot disturb their flow and interrelationship without lessening or even harming the director's intent. Where the alien hand that dare touch what has been called by Denis Marion in his monograph on Stroheim* "one of the most beautiful love scenes in the cinema" (the first meeting of Nicki and Mitzi in the garden)— "Never has such a scene been done with such discretion . . . the moonlight, the abandoned coach, the apple-blossoms, the exquisite modesty of the scene in which the sole caress permitted the man consists of draping his officer's cloak around the shivering young girl"? Is it not an eclogue, a pastoral poem between the two? And so this scene was not touched in Part One. The bordello sequence was considerably reduced but it "plays" even

*"Erich von Stroheim wrote sound novels in the silent days." (Jean-Luc Godard).

*Etudes cinématographiques, No. 48-50 (Paris: Lettres Modernes, 1966).

with this reduction. So that what is most precious to the film is what could least be tampered with—its tact—in the two love scenes in the garden of Part One.

The Wedding March, a work seeped in Jansenism—predestination—postulates the denial of free will. Man, though depraved, is unable to resist God's grace. Joel Finler in his monograph on Stroheim* rightly points out that "just as *Foolish Wives* marked the peak of his early career as director, *The Wedding March* is the high point of his maturity. Never, apart from *Greed,* has his direction been so sure."

In it he evoked the figurative myth of the "gay Vienna" of pre-World War I during the fading light of the Austro-Hungarian Empire, a light in fact still so roseate that in its dusk it seemed to Stefan Zweig like "the Age of Golden Security, a sweet time to be alive." Even Winston Churchill, looking back on it in *The World Crisis,* could say that "nations and empires, crowned with princes and potentates, rose majestically on every side, lapped in the accumulated treasures of the long peace. All were fitted and fastened, it seemed securely, into an enormous cantilever. The two mighty European systems [England and Germany] faced each other, glittering and clanking in their panoply, but with a tranquil gaze. . . . The old world, in its sunset, was fair to see." And apropos the pomp and circumstance of the Corpus Christi scene in the film, we have James Laver's observation (in his *Edwardian Promenade*) that it was "probably the last period in history when the fortunate thought

Stroheim (London: Studio Vista, 1967).

they could give pleasure to the others by displaying their good fortune before them."

And so, Stroheim evoked the Vienna of that age, which must surely seem to us today like a thousand years ago, in the same way that Canaletto and Guardi brought to completion the figurative myth of eighteenth-century Venice—or as Watteau did the Versailles gardens of Louis XIV.

As for the dusk on the eve of World War I, before the lights of Europe went out, bringing the romance of *The Wedding March* to an abrupt end, the war that ensued was to slaughter ten million men and maim twenty million more to decide which vultures were to rule the world.

Did Prince Nicki come back?

In *Merry Go Round,* Stroheim's precursor to *The Wedding March,* Prince Franzi comes back minus a leg, reduced to selling shoelaces and postcards in the Prater, now that the monarchy was gone. And the Prince's bride, the Princess Gisela, with whom he had entered into a loveless marriage of convenience by order of the Emperor, has now taken to the streets. The Prince and Mitzi, the girl he truly loved, pass without seeing each other. They never see each other again. This was the bitter ending of Stroheim's original script which he was not permitted to film. He never filmed the ending of *The Wedding March* either. Truly his wish to make a film of his native Vienna was jinxed. "But," as he was to say years later, "as you see, I am not easily discouraged." Indeed, he was not, for he tried again, for a third time, with *La Dame Blanche.* This one got as far as a detailed script, with Jean Renoir set to write the dialogue, Jacques Becker to act as assistant, and with Louis Jouvet and Jean-Louis Barrault selected as two of the stars. Stroheim himself was also set for a role. A producer was found, the financing was set—and then World War II broke out and that was the end of that. After that, he didn't try anymore—luck was against him and the wall was found to be harder than one's head. There were other projects—many of them, right up to the very end—but never again an attempt to evoke the old *Kaiserstadt*, Imperial Vienna.

La Dame Blanche was the last of Stroheim's trilogy of the Austria of the Hapsburg dual monarchy. I have read the script, but Denise Vernac, executrix of von Stroheim's estate, condensed it in a letter to the Italian critic and historian, Giulio Cesare Castello, published in a monograph on von Stroheim by *Bianco e Nero* in Rome in 1959.* She tells it well.

"La Dame Blanche—the ghostly form of a white lady—appears mysteriously every time tragedy strikes the Hapsburg dynasty, whose members personify Austria during the period in which the film is set—1888–1919.

"Through three families whose destinies are intertwined—the Hapsburgs, the family of an old nobleman who is the Emperor's master of the hunt and whose passion is raising eagles, and the family of a baker whose duty it is to supply semmels (rolls) for the Emperor's breakfast table—we witness Austrian life on all levels of society and enjoy the lively comments of old Augustin, the only one unhurt by the succession of catastrophes and who, possessing nothing, is at least rich in experience.

"The baker works for the Emperor and makes bread for his table, but the baker's son plots against the Emperor and uses this bread to try to poison the monarch. The baker's daughter, torn between duty and sisterly love, rushes to the palace to reveal the plot. There she meets the son of the Emperor's master of the hunt and an impossible love between them begins—a counterpart of that between the Crown Prince Rudolph and his mistress, the Baroness Maria Vetsera. First appearance of the 'white lady.' Was the old Emperor poisoned? No, but Rudolph committed suicide along with Maria Vetsera. Doom of impossible loves.

"The master of the hunt wants his son to marry a rich heiress. His property has become a burden, and his passion for raising eagles in captivity and for promoting hunting has swallowed up the family fortune.

"The baker refuses to forgive his son and forbids his daughter to see her lover. Discord reigns in the families.

"The captive eagles fight each other.

"A tacit revolt reigns in Austria.

"The 'white lady' again appears. The Empress is assassinated. The old Emperor is crushed by this new blow of fate.

"The Emperor wants to know what his people think. He questions the baker's son.

*A detailed transcript of the first two sequences of *La Dame Blanche*, plus eleven pages of drawings by Stroheim of uniforms and accessories required for the production and a complete breakdown of all the costumes, uniforms and accessories required for the film appears in this publication also.

Each listens to the other's point of view and understands what separates them. There is no way to resolve the differences, however, but the Emperor pardons the young anarchist. The baker's daughter, victim of a stupid incident, disappears in order to hide her disgrace. The master of the hunt's son is desperate.

"Third appearance of the 'white lady.' Sarajevo.

"The baker's son and the master of the hunt's son join the army, one knowing that he is going toward disaster but obeying a family tradition, the other believing that, as a result of the war, 'things will finally change.'

"The old Emperor is more than ever alone. This time the apparition is seen soaring over Vienna. It is a catastrophe for the whole of Austria. The war is lost.

"The master of the hunt dies and the only inheritance he leaves his son is an old dying eagle and an eaglet. Will his son be able to help the eaglet survive? The symbol is clear.

"The baker's son has returned a cripple. He sells shoelaces and pencils on a street corner. But things have really not changed so much. His sister finds the master of the hunt's son again. In all this tumult, love alone has gained some rights. On the horizon, which the lovers contemplate over the roofs of Vienna, the apparition fades away as the dawn breaks.

"Will Austria know better days?"

Stroheim, besides directing the film from his own script, was to have also played the master of the hunt, Louis Jouvet that of his inseparable friend, a Cistercian monk, and Jean-Louis Barrault was to have been the baker's son.

Would there have been a *Wedding March* if Stroheim had been permitted to complete *Merry Go Round*? One can believe it or not. The stories are basically similar with points of difference. . . .

A prince attached to the Hapsburg court of pre-1914 falls in love with a girl of the people who works in the carousel concession of the Prater, where her father is a puppeteer. But the prince is forced by the emperor to enter into a loveless marriage of convenience with a countess. The war breaks out, he goes to the front, and comes back a cripple. The terrible postwar inflation and end of the monarchy have forced the countess into the streets. The prince becomes a beggar. He and his true love never meet again. In *Merry Go Round*, Mitzi (it's always Mitzi) has a boyfriend, too, who hopes to marry her, a hunchback who tends the gorilla cage in the Prater. And the Countess, though affianced to the prince, is carrying on with her groom. Both films began the same way, in the morning with the waking of the prince, and in both films the prince meets his little Mitzi by chance—Nicki in front of St. Stephen's on Corpus Christi Day and Franz in the Prater. Nicki is forced by his father to enter into a loveless marriage of (financial) convenience and Franz is forced by the emperor to enter a similar marriage of (political) convenience. A wine-garden becomes the rendezvous of the lovers in *The Wedding March*, the Prater, the people's amusement park, their rendezvous in *Merry Go Round*. In both scripts, the prologues, introducing Vienna as a city of contrasts, gay and sad, are strikingly similar. Joseph Wechsberg in his Johann Strauss biography makes a point of this when he says, "The Viennese can be very amusing, very merry and gay, but they also have spells of depression. Freud understood this. It is no accident that he developed his theories in Vienna."

In any case, we have as a legacy a trilogy, but a maimed trilogy — three complete scripts, *Merry Go Round*, *The Wedding March* and *La Dame Blanche*, and two fragmentary films, *Merry Go Round* and *The Wedding March*.

Nobody marries for love in *The Wedding March*, only for what can be got out of it: Prince Nicki to Cecelia, for her munificent dowry that will accrue to the broke Wildeliebe-Rauffenburgs, Cecelia to Prince Nicki for the title Princess, and Mitzi to Schani to keep him from killing Nicki . . . true Austrians all . . . *tu, Austria, nube* . . . "thou, Austria, marry." . . .

When Nicki, at a rendezvous with Mitzi, gives the watchdog in the garden beneath her window a string of sausages to quiet his barking, it echoes the string of sausages that Schani munched earlier, waiting for the start of the Corpus Christi procession, which busied him, too, while Nicki flirted with his girl, Mitzi, then as he is about to do again now. (Talk about details — even the dog has a romantic purpose, his kennel being set amid a bower of white flowers.) And when Schani in a rage at not being able to win Mitzi's affection tears off a branch of apple blossoms, breaks it and throws it in impotent fury on the ground, it evokes the memory of Nicki, after his first meeting with Mitzi that first night in the garden, tenderly breaking off a sprig of the blossoms and inhaling their fragrance as a souvenir of their encounter. And is not the Iron Man carrying off the naiad from the Danube echoed by Nicki carrying the frightened Mitzi, who has seen this apparition? The Iron Man will have his will with the nymph as Nicki has already had his with Mitzi.* *The Wedding March* is full of details like these, of parallels like these, and they are very characteristic of the director's penchant for ironic contrast. When Prince Nicki visits the wine-garden for the first time, his introduction to the inner court under the apple blossoms is a sow being contentedly suckled by a brood of her young. The director makes the odor palpable. And when Nicki talks to Mitzi beneath her window the night of their second rendezvous, the love scene is preceded by Mitzi suddenly becoming aware of her underpants hanging on the line and quickly snatching them off in embarrassment. The ladder that Nicki raises to her window is, as Freddy Buache pointed out, a phallic symbol, as is the rearing up of the stallion on which Prince Nicki is mounted in the Stefansplatz, which becomes an aggressive sexual act to which the virginal Mitzi reacts in an unforgettable close-up of its erotic effect on her.

(He got every effect he wanted at a time when there was no such thing as a "permissive" screen, when censorship was as strict [and, alas, often as stupid] as it could be, a fact

*The dual crest of the Wildeliebe-Rauffenburg family escutcheon before the front pew in St. Stephen's shows a satyr grasping a nymph next to the coat-of-arms.

of life that sophisticated directors like Stroheim, Pabst, Lubitsch and von Sternberg learned to live with but which enforced subtlety on them. Who, once having seen it, does not remember the sardonic innuendo of the she-goat backing up practically in Karamzin's face as he gazes lasciviously in a pocket mirror at the ambassador's wife taking off her wet clothes in *Foolish Wives*? Or the slow pan up the idiot girl as Karamzin regards her, with the rent in the skirt of her dress so tellingly placed as to allow of only one interpretation for what is in Karamzin's mind?)

Stroheim has always been felicitous in the choice of names for his characters. Just as the Elizabethan and Jacobean theatres and those of Congreve, Sheridan, Wycherly, John Gay, and Goldsmith gave names to their personages that described their characters, idiosyncrasies or professions, Stroheim in *The Wedding March,* for instance, calls his aristocratic family not after such recognized names as the Lichtensteins, Schwarzenbergs, Potockis, Esterházys, Czernins or Hohenlohes, but gives them one of his own devising, a parody, in fact, on old aristocratic Austrian names, the Wildeliebe-Rauffenburgs, if you please, "the rough-house wild lovers." There was a Laufenburg estate in the early thirteenth century from which Rudolph II of Hapsburg descended from the house of Hapsburg-Laufenburg (another instance of aggrandizement through marriage ..."*Du glückliches Österreich, heirate...*") Schweisser, whose fortune was made making and selling corn-plasters (there is nothing like catering to just about everyone, is there?) has a name that literally means "one who sweats" (did not Dostoievski call the bastard son of Karamazov *père* "Smerdyakov"—just as literally, "Stinker Jake"?). The Schrammels (Mitzi and her father, Martin), being musicians in the wine-garden, are generically named after the popular Viennese vocal or instrumental ensembles which sang or played (in very close harmony) folksongs.

Are there any more Mitzis still in Vienna? Why not? There may not be any more Wildeliebe-Rauffenburgs or Laufenburgs or Hohenlohes, but there will always be Schweissers—and Mitzis. She is the sweet young thing, the pretty *Wienerin* incarnate. Empires may crumble and kingdoms fall, but the Mitzis (and the Schweissers) go on forever. As do their counterparts in all the countries of the earth.

So, in a milieu of the world of Hogarth and Goya, von Stroheim placed his principal characters, the *süsse Mäd'ln* and the rakehell heroes (whether their names were Franzi, Danilo, Nicki, or Wolf [Wolfram, "Wild" Wolfram of *Queen Kelly*]), the cosmopolitan Middle Europe (which in World War I became the Central Powers, with the Germany of Kaiser Wilhelm II at their head), a world of grandees and diamantine luxury in which Prince Nicki was but one of the many scions of noble families whose escutcheons by 1914 were not only cracked but crumbling. It was for as long as it was possible for it to be a world of *"Küss' die Hand, gnädige Frau,"** "Melde gehorsamst!"†* and *"Hab acht! Recht schaut!"‡*

*"I kiss your hand, dear lady."
†"At your service, sir!"
‡"Atten—tion!... Eyes right!"

The artist takes reality and by his personal vision of it transfigures it. In the process he creates a work of art. Without poetry as the goal in this transfiguration, no matter what else the artist accomplishes, there is no art. The luxurious sets that Pat Powers's hundreds of thousands of dollars paid for in *The Wedding March* (or Carl Laemmle's paid for in *Foolish Wives*) would have been for nothing if a poetic impulse were lacking. It is this that I seek not only in films but in writings about films—the search for these values, such as the kind I find in painting and the writings about paintings, especially by the painters themselves, like Picasso's "Paintings have always been made as princes made children—with shepherdesses. One never makes a portrait of the Parthenon; one never paints a Louis XV chair." By which he meant that beauty is what the artist makes of it. "Nothing in itself is beautiful," said Nietzsche; "man alone is beautiful." Once, while painting a rooster, Picasso said to a friend watching him, "Roosters—we've always had roosters, but, like everything else in life, we must discover them. Just as Corot discovered the morning and as Renoir discovered little girls." Or Cocteau speaking of Venice, "...where the horses live on the cornices, where the lions fly from one column to another, and where, on the contrary, the pigeons walk gravely about the square, wearing carnival costumes and holding their hands behind their backs."

To see freshly like that...

As Knut Hamsun did when he referred in *Pan* to "the can-can of humanity"...the same Hamsun who could move from so sardonic an observation to his anecdote (in the same novel) of the man at a ball who asks a seated girl to dance and she shakes her head and he repeats the request, to which she replies, "Can you imagine, my father was so handsome and my mother a perfect beauty, and my father took my mother by storm—but I was born lame."*

Why do I tell this? To imply that the anecdote is worthy of Stroheim? Or vice versa? It doesn't matter. What matters is that Stroheim equaled it in his own anecdote (in *Foolish Wives*) of the "rude" American officer who twice ignores an object dropped by the ambassador's wife and after ignoring it a third time is discovered by the now contemptuous woman to be armless under his cape. Stroheim's blast at the atrocity of war.

And the "casting" of the actor for this role of the armless marine! Where did he ever find such a face? The late Duke of Windsor, when he was Prince of Wales, once, during World War I, at a base hospital in France, insisted, against admonishments made to him, on going into a room harboring a "basket case"—quadruple amputee, deaf, dumb and blind—achieved in the service of King and Country. He emerged weeping. If such a victim of war could still be said to have a face it might have looked like the face of the double amputee marine officer in *Foolish Wives*. Do you know the marvelous black-and-white line drawings illustrating the Socratic irony of Hašek's odyssey of *The Good Soldier Schweik*, that "bit-

*Cecelia in *The Wedding March*, for all her millions, has a clubfoot.

terly hilarious book''?* Look at the drawing of the fierce Austrian officer with the *Schnurrbart*† who is interrogating the baby-faced Schweik, as limned by the artist, Josef Lada — then look at Prince Nicki's father, Ottokar, an absolute dead-ringer Junker tyrant.

True artists think alike. . . .

Mordaunt Hall, erstwhile film critic of the New York *Times* (indeed, its first one to sign his reviews) did a "review" of Stroheim's *The Merry Widow* so full of non sequiturs that one felt one was losing one's mind trying to read it. But at one point he hits on what seems like a revelation when he describes the director as having "an Emile Zola–Elinor Glyn complex." He is "warm," as we used to say in that hide-and-seek game we once played, but he's still wide of the mark. He'd have been closer to say that it looked as if the Marquis de Sade had written *Graustark*.

But the fact is that Stroheim's films were never set in "Elinor Glyn or Anthony Hope or George Barr McCutcheon country," which is to say in the Never-Never-Lands so beloved of Hollywood like Graustark, Ruritania, Sylvania and the like. They were set in real places, the Dolomites, Paris, Vienna, Montenegro. Even the principality of "Kronberg" in *Queen Kelly* is a thinly disguised Duchy of pre–World War I Prussia, one of the Imperial Duodec States before the unification of Germany. Not to mention such real American places as San Francisco and New York, which also served as backgrounds for him. And what could be "realer" than Death Valley?

Remains:
A word about color and music . . .

He had always been interested in color, even when all films were in black and white, as far back as the 1919 *Blind Husbands,* where he hand-tinted the flames in a candelabra, an effect he repeated in the 1922 *Foolish Wives,* plus hand-tinting the flames that envelop the tower of the villa in the fire scene at the end, and, of course, the gold-tinting of all gold and quasi-gold objects throughout *Greed.* In *The Wedding March* the prologue (cut from the film) originally showed the family crest of the Wildeliebe-Rauffenburgs in color (with, the charming, but for 1926* incredible, indication in the script of the scene to be accompanied by the *sound effect* of doves, fluttering about, cooing). The Corpus Christi procession was, of course, shot in full color to make vivid the pomp and pageantry of the spectacle, and the bordello sequences were indicated in the script to be printed on red-tinted film stock (which was not done). (It isn't as if he wasn't trying to make his films as expressive as he possibly could. It was that he was an anomaly to the Hollywood producers from the very beginning, a nonconformist, always wanting things that no one else ever called for and, hence, an odd duck. Ultimately he paid the penalty for scorning the "studio system." At this point it should be stated that he was the victim of his

*Alfred Polgar, Berlin critic of the 1920s.
†Mustache, usually a large one.

*The script was written in 1926.

own *daemon*. Hollywood, the worst place to nurture his visions, was the only place that could afford them. Surely, the irony was not lost on him. He never could have produced his expensive films in Europe.)

Many years later I was driving up Fifth Avenue in New York with him one rainy night when the long ribbon of green traffic lights suddenly changed to red, like a necklace of emeralds become one of rubies, reflected in the glistening asphalt. "That would make a nice shot in a film," he said.

Stroheim's early use of color (such as, the hand-tinted coloring of frames or portions of frames) was in a real sense to be echoed years later when Eisenstein (a deep admirer of Stroheim) postulated the theory that color should be used like music in films—sparingly. "Music is good when it is necessary," he said, "and so should it be with color, to be used only when necessary. Not the colored film but color as color, for its own sake."

Music . . . sister art to the cinema . . .

There surely is a guardian angel in Heaven who watches over the music scores of films where it is important that the music be "just right." When one thinks that the music one has come to associate with one's favorite films might, by the merest chance, have been entrusted to someone else, it is—just unthinkable. Imagine anyone else's music other than Chaplin's for *City Lights* or *Modern Times* or Raoul Moretti's for *Sous les Toits de Paris* or Georges Auric's for *À Nous la Liberté* or Prokofiev's for *Alexander Nevsky* or Hugo Reisen-

feld's for *Tabu* or coming closer to our own time, Jean Constantin's for *The Four Hundred Blows,* one of the most haunting of all film scores. Who, having heard it played "live" by a full orchestra at the Astor in 1925, will ever forget the Mendoza-Axt score for *The Big Parade*? Chance was also on the side of *The Wedding March* in 1927 when the photoelectric cell had already been invented that could transmute sound waves into light waves and thereby make possible the synchronizing of musical scores on the films' sound tracks. And the guardian angel in charge of film music in Heaven must surely have smiled when it saw to it that one, J. S. Zamecnik, and another, Luis de Francesco, were chosen to do the music. Who, once having heard this beautiful score, could countenance the thought of anyone else's music for it—could even watch the film (a silent one, after all) without it? Music was never more an integral part of the film than in the case of the Zamecnik–de Francesco score for *The Wedding March.* "*Wo Worte nicht mehr hinreichen, sprechen die Tone,*" said another of Vienna's sons, the poet-playwright Grillparzer. "Where words can no longer reach one, music speaks. What images can no longer convey is portrayed by its sounds. Unutterable yearnings and silent longings, love's desire, that overweening sadness in search of its cause that is afraid to find it lest it be in one's self, the faith that soars, inarticulate prayers that falter, all that is beyond words and images, belongs to the domain of music."

Let the sons of Vienna speak, for here is another, the philosopher Wittgenstein, with "The unsayable alone is important. All that really matters in human life is precisely what we must be silent about." This is the role of music, this is the role that the Zamecnik-de Francesco score for *The Wedding March* fills, that all the beautiful music scores for the films fill, because when the writer and director can go no farther, the composer or arranger takes it from there and delivers it to us. That is the function of music—the greatest art.

Summing up . . .

There is a painting by Degas, who always painted with exquisite tact, called "The Curtain Falls," which does, indeed, catch the curtain at a ballet performance in a theatre in the process of coming down as behind it and still partly visible on the stage can be seen the dancers in their final whirl. Three arts meet at this magical moment—painting, theatre and music—here, indeed, are the "voices of silence" of Malraux. Do you not hear the music's peroration of the dance? What was it Keats said? "Heard melodies are sweet,/ but those unheard are sweeter. . . ." Degas' ability to capture movement which is completed by the beholder was a characteristic mark of his sensibility. Note that I don't say virtuosity for, though he had it *in excelsis,* he never put it to the service of effect for the sake of that effect. Here is a painting done with logic and style, but the style comes from the logic, it is not imposed or grafted upon it; here style becomes the servant of meaning. The subject

here in itself is not important, as the subjects of so much in the graphic arts are not, but the exaltation deriving from its treatment *is* of the highest importance (*vide* the paintings of Soutine). Jean-Luc Godard put it another way when he described the shots of Rossellini as being "not true because they are beautiful but beautiful because they are true"—so apt in the case also of von Stroheim that I can recall none other that puts more succinctly his method that eschewed all tricks and effects for the sake of effects, whose sensibility would not permit any indulgence in theatrical "shock effects," not even the movement of the camera if it was unnecessary. There are only a few brief camera movements in the whole of *The Wedding March* (such as the pan from Mitzi's hands playing the harp up to her face)—the "punctuation" being achieved, as in *Potemkin,* by the cut. There is nothing wrong with this method of telling a story filmically and it is still as effective today as it was in 1915 when Griffith used it so tellingly in *The Birth of a Nation.* It has never been improved upon as film structure, despite rare digressions like *The Last Laugh* with its eloquent use of the subjective moving camera. And while it may be said that *The Wedding March* is in direct line of descent from the lyricism of the 1919 *Broken Blossoms* of Griffith and the 1921 *Four Horsemen of the Apocalypse* of Rex Ingram, both of which relied totally on the cut for their syntax, it is a far more sophisticated work than either, despite the similarity of their techniques, the basic simplicity of their stories, and the surface resemblance of their styles. It is as far from the operatic chop-suey and bombast of the early Cecil B. de Mille as it could be.

But true artists think alike. . . .

Five years before Murnau's opening shot in *Sunrise* of the train poster melting via a dissolve into an exact shot of the same train, Stroheim had indicated at the beginning of *Merry Go Round* that it was to open with still photos of Vienna — the Rathaus, St. Stephen's, etc. — each dissolving into actual shots of those places. The blindfolded musicians in the *maison de rendezvous* in *The Merry Widow* can be found in Casanova's memoirs, whereas the baroque bedroom of the mad queen in *Queen Kelly*, with its sculptured cupids ringing the bed on a raised dais, black draperies and white marble columns, had nothing on its real-life counterpart, that of the French actress Gaby Deslys in her house in London's Kensington where her elaborate bed sprawled on a dais beneath an arch of black marble supported by white marble pillars. Pabst (another admirer of Stroheim) ended his romantic *L'Atlantide* with the Foreign Legion officer going off into the desert in a sandstorm to find his heart's love, the beauteous Antinea — and Stroheim ends his equally romantic *Wedding March* with Prince Nicki going off into a bleak future in a rainstorm, having lost his heart's love, pretty little Mitzi.

In the morass of so many unspeakable films of today, it may seem strange to be reminded that films once looked upon women with adoration. In Rex Ingram's *Mare Nostrum*, after Blasco Ibañez, there is a marvelous shot of the Triton at night watching, enthralled, the goddess Amphitrite plunging her white chargers through the moonlit waves from her conch shell. And in *L'Atlantide*, Pabst's poetic fantasy after Pierre Benoit, Count Bielowski, raving over the beauty of the white queen, Antinea, who rules the domain in which the Legionnaire officer, Saint-Avit, finds himself a captive beneath the Sahara, says she is as beautiful as a goddess. "A goddess?" repeats Saint-Avit, incredulously. "Why not?" answers the Count. "Are not all women in some way divine?"

We are a long way from that today, a long dismal way.

As Pascin was an entomologist of women, Stroheim was an entomologist of the human race. To the query: why, if he was such a romantic, were his stories so cruel, the bleakness of his stories must echo him who said, "I have a heart but my heart has no heart." This refractory genius who insisted on having his own way, was he not archetypical of those few stubborn men like him who also insisted, as a result of which we have an art of the film at all? Certainly the motion pictures never started out to be an art but an industry, as profitable as the Hollywood solons and satraps could make it. There were two ways a director could find favor with the studios which controlled production: pander to the mob on the lowest mental level to insure the greatest possible box-office returns — or — indulge in the "high tessitura" of a Sternberg or Ophuls, which involved virtuoso technique put to the service of high-powered stars. Stroheim chose a third. And just as it isolated him among all other directors of his time, it isolates him today on Parnassus. The Chinese have a proverb, "You can know the skin of a tiger but not his bones," by which they mean you can know the face of a man but not his heart. Dostoievski was as misunderstood by his contemporaries and as isolated for it as Stroheim was to become. What they said of the author of *The Brothers Karamazov* was to be said of the director of *Greed* and *The Wedding March*. He was rich in talent, they admitted, but poor in discipline; they praised his originality and ability to breathe life into his characters but damned his semi-hysterical overtones, grotesque touches, and morbid types laid out under the microscope. And if Dostoievski's works are deeply religious, obsessed with man's search for faith after abandoning true Christianity, Stroheim's seem to say, along with Jules Renard, "I don't understand life at all, but I don't say it is impossible that God may understand it a little."* "There are moments of insight," continued Renard, "which can only stem from absolute honesty of perception added to complete largeness of spirit." The episode of the armless marine in *Foolish Wives* was one such. The scene between Schweisser and Cecelia after his return home in the early morning after a night of drunken debauchery at Madame Rosa's is another. The dissipation is still on his face (and in a closeup Cecelia notices that one of his shirt studs is unbuttoned, a minute detail that says it all), but joy is in his heart as he tells her

of the arrangement made with Prince Ottokar that will unite Cecelia and Prince Nicki in marriage. "But I have never even met the Prince," says Cecelia.

"You will — soon," says her father.

"How could he be in love with me?" asks Cecelia.

"You have twenty millions," says her father. "Money couldn't make a man feel love," she replies.

"Don't be a silly goose," says her father. "Love will come — in time." Then he adds, happily, "Princess Cecelia — doesn't that sound nice?"

"A limping Princess," says Cecelia, at which her father, as a flood of compassion breaks over him, embraces her, hugging her, covering her face with kisses. . . . Stroheim then juxtaposes this scene of great tenderness with its opposite at the Wildeliebe-Rauffenburgs', a scene of pure sarcasm on the same subject. "I presume you even proposed to the young lady," says Prince Nicki to his father. "Or did you leave that insignificant detail to me?"

"Did it ever occur to you," he continues, "that I might be in love with someone else?"

"*You*, in love?" explodes his father incredulously, to which he adds, "You idiot!"

"Of course," says Nicki, taking in his father and mother, "you two wouldn't know, but some people *do* fall in love, really!"

"But marriage," says Nicki's mother smiling, "is *one thing* and love *another!*" Then turning to her husband, sweetly, "*N'est-ce pas*, Ottokar?"

"I'm tired of this nonsense," shouts Prince

*The Journal of Jules Renard, edited and translated by Louise Bogan and Elizabeth Roget (New York: George Braziller, 1964).

Ottokar; "I command! The wedding will be the first of June!"

"How dare he talk to me that way!" says Nicki.

"But Nicki...," cajoles his mother, sitting on his lap, endearingly, "this would mean *so much* money!"

"How much?" asks Nicki.

"A huge fortune," she says.

"Seems to me that girl limps on both legs!" concludes Nicki, which leaves his mother laughing. Then comes the confessional scene with Mitzi in St. Stephen's. "Confess yourself to Heaven," says the title. And as Mitzi does, in a corner almost unseen, the sacristan with his hot iron, by pressing down on the melted wax dripping from the candles, absorbs the sin and suffering of the abandoned young woman. This was a relic of old Vienna, already a dead thing, extinct as if it had never existed, by the time (1926) Stroheim decided he was ready to make his film, to recreate the atmosphere, physical and moral, of the old Hapsburg monarchy. Phoenix-like it would rise in Hollywood from the ashes left by the awful years of holocaust that had engulfed it scarcely eight years before. He had eight years to think it over.

The Chinese have excelled in landscape painting since the early eighth century. Chinese artists used to travel great distances to spend hours and days contemplating a famous site, but they did not paint until they were back in their studios, after memory had performed its magical decanting operation, eliminating nonessentials and leaving only beauty.

This is how Stroheim recreated the old Vienna of his memory, Vienna with its slow waltz rhythms, its splendors and its miseries. It is no easy thing to be a historian. A. F. Pribram, the Austrian historian, told C. A. MacCartney, a don at All Souls College at Oxford, that he gave up trying to do research for a history of Austria because he knew only fourteen languages. MacCartney himself speaks of the severe rationing that affected Vienna during the first World War, not only at home but at the front. In one unit of the army, he recalled, there were uniforms sufficient just for men at the front lines. Those in reserve units had to wait in their underwear. This is better than the ridiculous anecdotes that dogged Stroheim about "monogrammed silk underwear for his soldiers" coined by press-agent harlots of the studios and repeated to liven up their prose by "historians" of the motion pictures. I said he waited eight years after the collapse of the Austro-Hungarian monarchy before he was ready to make *The Wedding March*. Actually, four years before, he had tried it with *Merry Go Round*—and again later with *La Dame Blanche*—which recalls what Penelope Gilliatt quotes Jean Renoir as once having said to her, speaking figuratively, "Probably everyone makes only one film in his life, then smashes it to pieces and makes it again."* Well, Stroheim didn't exactly smash his own films (others did that for him only too well) but each time he tried anew he added touches, nuances, refining it. His chief characteristic being ironic

*Unholy Fools: Wits, Comics, Disturbers of the Peace (New York: Viking, 1973).

contrast, he juxtaposed the sacred and profane in close proximity and against each other, his films swinging in polarity between the two, between the forces of good and evil. Not for him, trick shots for their own sake, meaningless camera angles *pour épater la bourgeoisie,* what Eisenstein called "unmotivated camera mischief" — every shot had to mean something that would add to the cumulative effect of the whole. He used the cut (rarely the dissolve — offhand I can remember it only twice, in *Greed,* from the crowded boardwalk to the vast gray sea, to connote Marcus's despair, and from a closeup of the eyes of a cat to one of Marcus Schouler [Jean Hersholt])* and "montage within the frame," so characteristic also of Eisenstein, apart from the latter's "linkage" montage, which was the juxtaposition of two or more shots to create an idea that did not exist apart from this juxtaposition, namely, Kerensky before the doors of the Czar's private chambers in the Winter Palace followed by a figure of Napoleon, another of a goddess holding forth a wreath of laurel, finally a peacock in full vainglorious feather (in *Ten Days That Shook the World*). A classic example of Eisenstein's "interior" montage, or within the frame (the composition itself), is to be found in a shot in *Thunder Over Mexico,* made from material filmed by him for his unfinished epic *Que Viva Mexico!* It shows a pekinese lolling on a saloon table under a portrait of the ruthless dictator, General Diaz, and a drunken officer

in a half stupor at the table — three items linked to get across one central idea, the complicity of the bourgeoisie with official corruption. In the same way does one of the drunken officers in the bordello in *The Wedding March* precariously swing a just-opened bottle of champagne, spurting its foam across the screen for an image bolder in its implication than could conceivably have been permitted literally under the censorship strictures of 1928. But they didn't need literalness of sex then; they had imagery — as Nora Desmond in *Sunset Boulevard* said of the silent films, "We didn't need sound — we had faces." Anyway, Stroheim's world was a man's world — there were no seductresses in his films, only seducers — no procurers, only procuresses. And the seducers came from the old legends that formed the matrix of the Hapsburg dynasty, upon which we have touched. Barthélemy Amengual in his essay "*Stroheim entre la legende et l'histoire*"* recalls Oswald Ducrot's saying, "Like Stroheim himself, his camera wears a monocle." Certainly the characters that people his films (from *Foolish Wives* on) have the swagger of those we see in the canvases of Toulouse-Lautrec, and he could etch the lines of a face with the same acidity. The two would have hit it off well, I am certain. His method was empirical in contrast to Eisenstein's, which was scientific, but in the end it was Stroheim whom Eisenstein held in the highest esteem among his fellow directors. Those two would have hit it off well, too,

*And a third time, in *The Merry Widow,* from a cold winter rain to frozen icicles to denote a passage of time. Even the dissolve had to have a purpose. The bordello dissolves in *The Wedding March* are not his, but the editors'.

Études cinématographiques, 48-50 (Stroheim) (Paris: Lettres Modernes, 1966).

though they never met. Their goals were different but their values were the same. The values of all artists are the same, that is the great fraternity of art. The times have nothing to do with it, though changing times and changing mores may reject some values once held high. Can one imagine a film of today being described as being like lace knitted by a chaste young girl, and this meant as a high compliment? And yet this is how Tolstoi described a short story by Chekhov. Another element of Stroheim's style which makes it so palatable is its playfulness (always excepting *Greed* — he was in dead earnest there) to such a degree that Eisenstein once said, "I can't always tell when he's serious or when he's kidding." He had a prodigious sense of humor and a withering wit. Compare the solemnity with which a director like Clarence Brown does *Flesh and the Devil* and the gaiety with which Stroheim did *The Merry Widow*. Both films dealing with Continental sex and soldiers derive from trivial sources and so it becomes wholly a matter of attitude and style as to what will come out of them. Brown, taking his material seriously, strides flatfooted through his contretemps, all of which we have to take on the director's say-so because nothing that happens convinces us. The leavening of humor that might have imparted a humanness to the characters is completely lacking. The trouble is that Brown goes along with his material, which becomes redundant, and redundancy is a bore. Stroheim works *against* his material and spoofs it without losing his' central "romantic franchise" with the infectiously happy result we

know. Brown's turns of plot are predictable at every step — Stroheim's are not at all and are, as often as not, bizarre. Hence the fun of discovery that exists in the film. Compare the wooden John Gilbert in *Flesh and the Devil* and the dash of the same actor in *The Merry Widow* — even Mae Murray (Heaven knows, no Duse) out-acts Garbo. Above everything, Stroheim was a director of actors and actresses who invariably gave unique performances under his direction which they were never able to duplicate under anyone else. He had no use for stars and only accepted Gilbert and Murray because MGM forced them on him. For *The Wedding March* he found a nineteen-year-old Los Angeles schoolgirl, Fay Wray, and made a star of her. As in *Foolish Wives* (and *Blind Husbands* before that), he took the romantic lead opposite Miss Wray himself. The two made a charming couple as the shy Mitzi and the worldly Prince Nicki, and their flirtation scene while he is on duty, mounted on his horse (before St. Stephen's while the crowd is waiting for the Corpus Christi procession) is one of the most delightful bits of byplay in the entire cinema repertoire. Here the silent and sound films meet and bow to each other, for neither Mitzi nor Prince Nicki can talk to the other and must preserve their decorum and the secrecy of their public flirtation, with the result that this long sequence, played entirely in pantomime, would have been played the same way even if *The Wedding March* were a sound film. I know of only one sequence to match it, in a French film, *Le Revenant*, a sound film, in which Louis Jouvet returns after a long absence to his native town where he is greeted by an old friend, Marguerite Moreno, who tells him all that has happened in his absence, to which Jouvet, by his expressions, shows his reactions. As Moreno finishes, she smiles at him and says, "Still as witty as ever!"—and he hasn't said a word. It was a tour de force of playing vis-à-vis by two virtuoso actors and is the perfect sound-film corollary to the flirtation scene in *The Wedding March*. Each made the most perfect use of its medium.

"Life is interesting," said Goethe, "wherever you touch it." Stroheim found interest even in the occult, astrology, fortune-tellers, extra-sensory perception, and the like. A favorite book of his was Charles Fort's *The Damned*, about unexplained natural phenomena. And though he did not make scientific excursions into parapsychology and phenomenology, he was fascinated by them and sometimes imbued his films with them, not to mention mysticism, such as the subtitle in *The Wedding March* just before Prince Nicki visits Mitzi, after her accident, in the hospital: "There is no such thing as accident. It is Fate—mis-named." (Eugene O'Neill did not believe in accidents either, calling such incidents "Kismet" or "Fate," terms he often applied both to somber events in his own life as well as in his plays.) What were both saying but echoing Edward Fitz-Gerald's paraphrase of Omar Khayyám, "Yea, the first Morning of Creation wrote/ What the last Dawn of Reckoning shall read." Stroheim had as deep a feeling for Hungarian gypsy life in his very "Stroheimesque" novel, *Paprika*, set in pre–World War I Hungary, as did the Hungarian-born Franz Lehár, composer of *The Merry Widow*, and he was as cosmopolitan, as "all things to all men," as Lehár was, Lehár who "to the Viennese always seemed Viennese, to the Hungarians a Hungarian, to the Czechs a Czech, to the Poles and Slovaks a Pole and a Slovak."* Indeed, the opening chorus of Act II of *The Merry Widow* operetta is an elegant Polish polonaise, followed by a mad, foot-stomping Hungarian csárdás, which in turn is followed by a plaintive gypsy *lassan*, perhaps the most ravishing of all gypsy slow movements in music. To top these three would take—a Lehár, who does it with Sonia's song, "Vilia." *Paprika*, published (in 1935) between the debacle that was his last directorial attempt, *Walking Down Broadway*, and his personal triumph in Renoir's *La Grande Illusion*, was a passionately written story of the tziganes, the proud Hungarian gypsies, detailing the brief odyssey of a girl-child born during a storm in the paprika fields who became a beautiful creature desired by all men and how this enchantment with which she was both blessed and cursed brought her to an early and violent end. It would have provided the perfect libretto for an operetta (by Lehár—why not?—hadn't he admired Stroheim's film of *The Merry Widow* and said that if he hadn't already written the music for it, Stroheim's film would have inspired him to do so?)—as well as for a screenplay for a film of it the director would have given his soul to make. He identified himself so fully with the Hungarian gypsies

*Bernard Grun, *Gold & Silver: The Life & Times of Franz Lehár* (New York: David McKay Co., 1973).

that Denise Vernac, the devoted companion of his last years in France, told me that she noticed that stray dogs never barked at him, as they never do at gypsies either, she said, they being outcasts, too, perhaps sensing one of their own. Stroheim, himself, over a bottle of Black and White (his favorite brand of scotch) told me of a gypsy custom of dropping banknotes in good-size denominations in the coffins of the dead so that in the next life they could buy themselves a drink now and then.

Returning to *The Wedding March,* let Richard Watts describe the situation Stroheim found himself in upon the completion (for all "practical purposes," according to P. A. Powers and Paramount) of the film. Thus he reported it in the late New York *Herald Tribune* of which he was motion picture editor at the time (1928): "When you consider the time and money spent by routine directors on routine feature films . . . it hardly seems that a film company should begrudge the expenditures on *The Wedding March* made by the man who is probably the greatest director produced by the oncoming cinema. When, in addition, he presented the producing group with two rather than one, the cry of extravagance (leveled at him) seems all the more surprising. Curiously, the offer of two pictures for the price of one was rejected and aliens were set to cutting *The Wedding March* to the required length. Since it may sound surprising that any frugal business firm should refuse such an offer, you may suspect the real trouble is that the latest von Stroheim work is not a good photoplay. Yet all of the advance evidence discounts such a thought and sug-

gests another reason for the rejection. The director, it appears, was paid not by the week but by the picture, and if his ideas for cutting up the work into two parts were followed, he would have to be paid a double salary. Only in so fantastic a field as the cinema would you credit such a motive. Yet the motion pictures have always been surprisingly quaint in their treatment of von Stroheim. For example, *The Merry Widow* was his most successful work, economically, and yet the director received practically no money from it. Though it has been big box office everywhere, the studio bookkeeping always works out so that von Stroheim's share of the profits is not excessive, to employ an understatement.* It is not the purpose of this polemic to suggest that von Stroheim despite the success of all his pictures, from *Blind Husbands* to *The Merry Widow,* is out of a job as a result of a cinema conspiracy. Yet it is hardly deniable that the First Director is being picked on by the 'movie' magnates. The cause is, I suspect, fairly easy to discern. The screen, used to turning out conventional, sure-fire, factory-made directors and players, is completely baffled when faced by an idea or a person outside of the routine. It is less than surprising, therefore, when the films fail to dig out a proper niche for a Betty Bronson, a Raymond Griffith, or an Erich von Stroheim. He is no doubt a difficult, excitable and temperamental person, less than easy to manage. His first interest is neither the saving

*He told me he had, according to his contract with MGM, 25 percent of the profits, of which he received nothing because they said his profits on the $4,500,000 grossed on *The Merry Widow* had been "eaten up" by the losses the company sustained on *Greed.* (H. G. W.)

55

of expense nor the use of box-office qualities in his work. He has within him a morbid, unhappy, possibly unhealthy, strain that, among other things, keeps him from being the idol of the magnates. And yet he is the most important, the most vital and the most significant motion picture director extant. He has made in *Greed* the finest of realistic films and in *The Merry Widow* the most delightful of romantic comedies. Today, however, he is discredited in the popular eye, and, what is more important, he is out of a job. That's motion pictures!''

Failing to get Jesse Lasky of Paramount to agree to a six-hour version (already cut down by Stroheim from twelve hours), to be shown in two parts of three hours each either on one evening or separately on two successive evenings, Stroheim found himself eliminated from further negotiations on the editing. Sternberg was called in, others were called in; eventually Lasky, to avoid a massacre by cutting a six-hour film to two, compromised by allowing the film to be cut into two parts anyway, though not by Stroheim: Part One (the release version in the United States) from 14,000 feet to some 10,000 and Part Two from 10,000 feet to 5,000 (plus 2,000 feet of recapitulation of Part One so it could pass as a ''complete'' film (this latter only for South American and European distribution). As in the case of *Greed*, the ''excess'' footage was destroyed, as the ''excess'' footage of all the Stroheim films was destroyed. But the mutilation of important film works is an old story, continuing to this day. It's only that Stroheim was the first victim. In recent years when the Shochiku Company

wanted to cut Kurosawa's *The Idiot* (after Dostoievski) from its four and a half hours to two, he told them, ''If you want to cut it, you'd better cut it lengthwise.'' (They went ahead, anyway, *but they preserved a negative of the complete version*.) Similarly they cut his *Seven Samurai* from three hours twenty minutes to approximately two and a half *(also preserving the negative of the complete version)*. Other Japanese films survived *in toto* despite their extreme length, such as the nine-and-a-half-hour three-part *Human Condition* of Kobayashi, and the four-hour *Chushingura*, to name two. In France there is a directors' syndicate or legislation that protects the director in this respect.* Hollywood affords its directors no such protection, although for a while some had it, by virtue of their stature, like Capra, Ford, Victor Fleming (when he directed the three-and-a-half-hour *Gone With the Wind*). But David Lean didn't have it when they reduced his *Lawrence of Arabia,* after its premiere showing, nor did Sam Peckinpah have it when MGM removed fifteen minutes from his *Pat Garret and Billy the Kid,* thus ''cutting the heart out

*Some other long films were the eight-hour Russian *War and Peace*, the seven-and-a-half-hour Italian *Aeneid*, the six-hour *Marius-Fanny-César* trilogy of Marcel Pagnol, the early *Dr. Mabuse* of Fritz Lang, running over four hours, the five-and-a-half-hour *Napoleon* of Abel Gance. More recently, the film of the O'Neill play *The Iceman Cometh* ran three hours and forty minutes. Didn't both Max Reinhardt and Erwin Piscator try in vain to obtain the Viennese satirist-critic Karl Kraus's permission to stage his vast antiwar play, *The Last Days of Mankind,* and fail because Kraus didn't think either would put it on for the ten evenings he said the full play would require? An abridged English translation was recently published in five acts and thirty-seven scenes, taking 237 pages, but the complete play ran to a hundred scenes and *800 pages*. (Kraus said that it was intended for ''a theatre on Mars''—theatre-goers in this world would not be able to endure it. Maybe the complete *Greed* and *The Wedding March,* though not so intended, fall into that category too.)

of the film," said the director, "by robbing the characters of their motivations." Speaking of the mutilation of *Lawrence of Arabia,* Stephen Farber, writing in the New York *Times,* excoriates the producers not only of Lean's film but of all directors who have suffered similar debasement of their work: "Why has it been done? Economics, of course; it will now be a little easier to run three shows daily and still get the last audience out before midnight. Exhibitors have a slightly shorter day, and maybe a little more popcorn can be sold. It is even possible that the executives at Columbia think they have improved the film by shortening it. This would not be the first — or last — time that business men have deluded themselves about their artistic sensitivity. But whatever their motives, they must be convinced that the people who see the movie won't know the difference or care. Their contempt for film is surpassed only by their contempt for the audience."

Here I would like to repeat a statement by von Sternberg, told me in connection with his role in the matter, that originally appeared in my study of him:* "As I recall, both of us, von Stroheim and I, were under contract to Paramount, though he had finished *The Wedding March* and edited it long before I was assigned to cut it down to releasable length. We were friendly, he had repeatedly expressed admiration for my work. The company had told him to cut it down so that it could be released and he said he could not. Thereupon it was suggested that others handle it, and, until my name was mentioned, he objected strenuously. He,

himself, showed me the film (to my recollection it included everything he intended to show). He asked me personally to take over the assignment, and I did so without any protest on his part. I told him precisely what I would shorten; we were friendly before, during and afterwards. . . . I showed him the shortened version and he thanked me. Had he objected to anything, I would not only have restored the film to its original length but would have refused to have anything more to do with it. I am explicit about this for it seems to be generally thought that I edited his work without his O.K. which is something I would not have done under any circumstances. . . . I had been strongly impressed with his earlier *Greed.* . . . I know nothing about the division of the film into two parts. I never saw the film again and how it was finally shown is unknown to me."

"The mark of genius," said V. S. Pritchett, "is an incessant activity. Genius is a greed for more."

It was one of Thomas Mann's cherished convictions that only the exhaustive was truly interesting.

"One must have chaos within himself to give birth to a dancing star." (Nietzsche, *Thus Spake Zarathustra*)

If genius is, indeed, an infinite capacity for taking pains, Stroheim qualified — in spades, as they say.

Jacob Roth, describing the marriage of the young Emperor Franz Josef to the beauteous Elizabeth of Bavaria, in his book *Radetzky March,* rhapsodizes that "above all heads a

Josef von Sternberg: A Critical Study (New York: E. P. Dutton, 1967).

heaven of melody soared, a canopy of black and gold notes...guns thundered in joyful salute, the organ pealed...." Sights and sounds whose echoes are found in *The Wedding March*—the salute of the guns as surely a harbinger of death for Elizabeth as it was to be for Cecelia, and the organ that pealed for Elizabeth's wedding day just as surely a portent of doom rather than joy, just as it was to be for poor Cecelia, poor Cecelia with her twenty millions.... As for the bells that also pealed out from the belfry of St. Stephen's for both of them, they were not wedding bells but a tocsin, and the hands that played the "Wedding March" on the organ were, indeed, as Stroheim showed them to be, skeletal hands....

What is it to be a philosopher? To see deeper into the human heart than anyone else? "The unsayable alone is important," said the Viennese philosopher Ludwig Wittgenstein. "All that matters in human life is just what we must be silent about." Thus we have parallel scenes at the conclusion of the films of two of the screen's supreme artists—Chaplin and Stroheim—scenes brushing the edge of pain, of one's happiness teetering on the brink of oblivion...the little tramp looking at the blind girl now no longer blind, thanks to him, at the close of *City Lights* and wondering, wondering if she will know him...and Nicki and Mitzi in the final moments of *The Wedding March* looking at each other outside the church after his marriage to Cecelia, looking at each other for a last agonizing moment.... In *Greed* the motivation was that not to have money was to be cheated out of life.... In *The Wedding March*

it is that not to have love is to be cheated out of life. Between the two, they just about say it all, don't they?

A friend of Toulouse-Lautrec once chided him during a night in one of his favorite haunts in Montmartre about the number of brandies he had imbibed that evening. "Some men can play the violin," replied Toulouse-Lautrec. "Some can paint—I can drink brandy." Then, almost as an afterthought, "And I can paint, too."

Stroheim could drink scotch and direct films, too, especially about the old Austro-Hungarian monarchy. *Paprika* is a film by Erich von Stroheim as sure as God made little fishes. Read the book, which is really a scenario, ready for shooting, and see for yourself. Nothing more vivid, more visual, more bursting with life was ever between covers. Maybe he felt, while writing it (he was unemployed at the time, following the contretemps about the cutting of *The Wedding March*), that even if it didn't get filmed it would at least exist as a film on the printed page.* After all, didn't all films start with the screenplay?

If Kreisler playing "The Old Refrain" or "Caprice Viennoise" had validity, Stroheim directing a film about this milieu had the same. Both were sons of Vienna, both knew exactly what they were doing. And each sang in his own way of:

"'s gibt nur a Kaiserstadt,

*As proof of his own regard for *Paprika*, it was dedicated by him to his mother. The only other work of his thus dedicated was *Greed*.

's gibt nur a Wien!''

*(There's but one Imperial city,
There's but one Vienna!)*

He was accused of going to extremes. But life is full of "corners" where extremes are to be found. His sets, elaborate as they sometimes were, were nowhere near as "wild" as the peacock throne of Ludwig II of Bavaria or the mural from the Winter Garden in the latter's Munich residence or his bedroom in the Linderhof Castle. But they were as beautiful as a canvas by Winterhalter, the Auersperg Palace, or the whirls and swirls of a silver breakfast coffee service by Hirsch & Smejda at the turn of the century. A realist, yes, but he knew, in the felicitous phrase of Cocteau, "how far to go too far." Never for a moment did he forget that the imagination of the audience is the director's finest asset and that he must know how to use it effectively. A satirist, yes, in almost everything he touched, reminding one of Horace's dictum that life being constituted as it is it was difficult *not* to be a satirist. I have a recurring dream of a film by von Stroheim in which one of the characters was the late Crown Prince Wilhelm Hohenzollern, "Willie," eldest son of Kaiser Wilhelm II of Germany during World War I. Chaplin caricatured him briefly and devastatingly in *Shoulder Arms,* but I was always curious to see how Stroheim would have delineated this tall, handsome, genial tennis-playing aristocrat, given to posing hand on hip, tête-à-tête or reviewing troops, with the stance of a real faggot which, of course, he wasn't (though it amused him to play at it for effect's sake, even though Papa didn't think it funny). Stroheim came near to the type in the Mlle. Fifi-like character (from Maupassant's "Boule de Suif") of the mincing Crown Prince Mirko in *The Merry Widow,* so vertiginously played by Roy d'Arcy with such a prodigality of sarcasm endowed him by the director. Here was Stroheim "having a ball," as they say, with Central European royal decadence before the guns of that fateful August 1914 called it a day.

Berlioz, despairing of his opera *The Trojans* ever being heard by anyone because of its length (five hours), as a precaution divided it into two parts, each of which could be performed separately, each complete in itself. *The Wedding March* was to be in that tradition. But Berlioz was luckier than Stroheim. *The Trojans* was at least performed that way, not often, to be sure, but at least preserved for such performances. *The Wedding March in toto* was not preserved. Part Two is totally lost. The case of Berlioz presents a striking parallel to that of von Stroheim. He, too, was a pioneer (of modern orchestration), he, too, was the subject of both abuse and acclaim throughout his life and long a figure of controversy. He, too, was criticized for the huge forces he employed—his *Grand Mass for the Dead* requiring, besides an expanded orchestra and a massive chorus, four brass bands. He, too, was thought to be crazy. He, too, after the failure of one of his operas, *Benvenuto Cellini,* didn't do another for eighteen years. (Stroheim's hiatus was longer. After the debacle of *Walking Down*

Broadway, his last work, twenty-five years passed and he *never* made another film.) And Berlioz, too, because his music didn't conform to the accepted canons of mid-nineteenth-century music-making, was considered something of an oddball. To Stroheim's screen-monocle he brandished his conductor's sword, literally—he conducted his *"Symphonie funèbre et triomphale"* (1840) in memory of the Paris Revolution of 1830 with a sword as his baton. He also had the same financial troubles. But this year, the Metropolitan Opera in New York performed his *Trojans* complete, and not in two parts, either, but, as its composer originally intended, all together, all five hours of it in one glorious evening.

More than words can say was the emotion one felt as the shimmering aria, "Nuit d'ivresse," soared once more from the stage describing the ecstatic night of the lovers, Dido and Aeneas, *"Nuit d'ivresse et d'extase infinie . . ."*—that Shakespearean love-duet, *"Par une telle nuit . . .,"* which recalls that moonlit night when Lorenzo and Jessica echoed Dido and Aeneas with "In such a night/ Troilus, methinks, mounted the Troyan walls,/ and sigh'd his soul toward the Grecian tents,/ where Cressid lay that night." And on such a night did Mitzi and Prince Nicki plight their troth in that swooningly beautiful first garden scene where Mitzi, approaching the broken carriage, commands it to take them for "a drive through paradise."

He was, after all, said the French critic, Marcel Martin, "the poet of love."

Another French critic, Barthélemy Amengual, placed him "with the Giottos of the screen—Méliès, Griffith, Feuillade, Sjøstrom and Chaplin."

Erwin Piscator found in *The Wedding March* "the richness of detail and characterization of Balzac."

Thomas Mann hoped Stroheim might bring *The Magic Mountain* to the screen, and Thomas Quinn Curtis, a mutual friend of both, brought them together in a real "nuit d'ivresse" for just this purpose but alas, alas, it was not fated to happen. . . .

"Anyone who will threaten to entertain you for twelve hours on end," wrote the eminent no-nonsense Scots critic and pioneer documentary filmmaker, John Grierson,* "is plainly in the grand manner. . . . *The Wedding March* became one of those traditional productions which company after company fail on. It soared into the millions. I saw great slices of it shot and great hunks of financiers' hair torn from the roots in the process. But not a frame of what I saw appeared in the final version. When Paramount bought and finished the film, Stroheim was on the outside as before. Yet for most of us Stroheim is the director of all directors, and I think largely because of his superlative disregard for the financiers who back him. . . . Surrounded by a thousand technicians and a thousand interests which conflict with his job of pure creation, a director has to have something of Lenin in him to come through. Strangely enough, there is not an

Grierson on Documentary, edited by Forsyth Hardy (New York: Praeger, 1971).

artist who ever appeared under him who will hear a word against von Stroheim. In a world of commercial flip-flap he does stand so surely for the larger intensities of art. . . . You do get something like a genuine picture of the man: when, standing dreadfully erect before the set, he screams, 'Cameras!' I have seen him do that . . . and I have seen him go off the hoop as he does subsequently, and be very much the blood-curdling creature of temperament. . . . It is worth seeing. He is the villain of the piece in this case, but you may believe with me that a single gesture of such villainy is worth a great deal of more flat-footed orthodoxy. 'What are a few deaths to the art of Benvenuto?'"

There were directors whose every new film was an event, a milestone in the history of the art. Murnau was one, Eisenstein another, Stroheim surely, and Chaplin, of course . . . the early Clair, Renoir, Lang, Griffith, and in our own time, Welles . . . Lubitsch, the "Americanized" Lubitsch, was facetious, though deliciously so, and Sternberg was hostile, though justifiably so. . . . In the cinema hierarchy magistral works in many colors within the medium existed without necessarily having to vie with *The Magic Flute* or *The Tempest* for immortality. . . .

He made a film, or tried to, as if it were an act of faith, utilizing the stratagems of dramaturgy invented by himself to make his statements, the mordant, brilliant, entirely personal satire of *The Merry Widow*, the bitter satire of *The Wedding March*. And just as *Don Quixote*

was the first modern novel and *Ulysses* the first revolutionary breakthrough, so was *The Birth of a Nation* the first modern film and *Greed* the first revolutionary breakthrough.

The nine films he made, or tried to make (one has to say it), were his own stations of the cross . . . *Blind Husbands, The Devil's Passkey, Foolish Wives, Merry Go Round, Greed, The Merry Widow, The Wedding March, Queen Kelly, Walking Down Broadway. . . .* These were his own Pleiades in the cinema firmament and, of the nine, the six that are visible (like their counterparts in the night sky) are *Blind Husbands, Foolish Wives, Merry Go Round, Greed, The Merry Widow,* and *The Wedding March.* Of the other three, one, *The Devil's Passkey,* being lost, is as invisible as the seventh star of the heavenly Pleiades, while the other two remain grotesque caricatures of their originals.

The loss of that portion of Stroheim's work which remains irretrievably lost is, of course, the first tragedy. The second and greater tragedy is the personal one for him, in whom the creative impulse was so strong and who had to content himself in his last years with writing novels and scripts which he envisioned as films, acting in other directors' films, but lying fallow in the thing he did best of all, as director. People have feelings—it's as simple as that. . . .

The attraction that the aesthetic sense has is a "pull" almost like that of gravity—at least for the creative impulse it is. Even a scientist can be so attracted. Copernicus, for example, was so moved by it in what can only be described as his mystical quest for a rationale in justifying his theory of the sun-centered planetary system, that he rhapsodized, "For in this most beautiful temple, who would place the lamp in another or better position than that from which it can light up the whole thing at the same time?" That's a pretty lyric flight for an astronomer.

So because he was an honest man besides being an artist, he repudiated all of his films that had been tampered with, which is to say all but the first two, *Blind Husbands* and *The Devil's Passkey*. As far as *The Wedding March* is concerned, the *Film Mercury*, an erstwhile Hollywood periodical edited by Tamar Lane in the twenties, carried the statement by von Stroheim: "I disclaim all responsibility for 'The Wedding March' in the form it is to be released by Paramount and had nothing to do with the picture in this form. I therefore do not wish my name to be associated with this picture."

"For in that day when those who follow us will be able to set a perspective on film history," wrote Jim Tully, fellow tippler and colleague in belles lettres of H. L. Mencken and George Jean Nathan, "Stroheim is likely to be considered the first man of genius and original talent to break his heart against the stone wall of cinema imbecility."

A desolate wind blows through the places in Hollywood where those wonderful old movie sets once stood, when studio craftsmanship reigned. Where is the splendor of Babylon and Hekatompylos? What remains of his sovereign art? "Die schönen Tage in Aranjuez," wrote Schiller in *Don Carlos*, "sind nun zu Ende."

(The beautiful days in Aranjuez have come to an end.)

At the end of Schnitzler's *Reigen*, the Count, coming out of his drunken stupor after he leaves the prostitute in the morning, pauses for a moment before the door downstairs. "Well," he muses, "it could have been beautiful, if I had only kissed her eyes. . . . It would have been almost an adventure . . . but . . . it wasn't to be. . . ." The line is a blossom plucked out of the mire. Which is what the love story in *The Wedding March* is.

Finally, we must pause to consider a reflection by Edward Dahlberg, on the man behind the artist. A long time ago (1937) I wrote, in another connection, "What strange destiny for a man! Is his name really Erich von Stroheim? Is he really a former lieutenant of the old Imperial Austrian Guard, the son of a great Bohemian nobleman? Is he not, rather, a creature from another world, marvelously possessed of a mysterious spirit, caparisoned to mystify the throng?" "It is the artist's legendary or apocryphal life that is important to him and his public," said Dahlberg. "His real life, however it may differ from the myth he has created about himself, is not necessarily interesting." It's like an artist's self-portrait. How can you quarrel with that? How he sees himself is part of what he is. You cannot separate the two, for they are superimposed, one upon the other.

"As with all geniuses," said Jean Renoir in an essay, "The Slave of His Creation,"* "Stroheim's field of effectiveness was not limited to the tool that fate had placed in his hands. Had

*Études cinématographiques 48-50 (Paris: Lettres Modernes, 1966).

he been born a hundred years before motion pictures he would have been a novelist or a musician but would have found some way to tell us what was on his mind. What is important in his case is that the world of his films is his exclusive creation.... Great artists honestly believe their work is that of a simple transcriber. They believe they are doing no more than recording the phenomena of the world that surrounds them when, in fact, they are absorbing what is essential, annexing it, and returning it to the public enriched by their own personality. It is finally this artist's truth that impresses itself upon history and becomes the true truth. Both *Greed*'s America and *The Merry Widow*'s Central Europe will remain the true expressions of the history and the geography of these places at the turn of the century. For if it is true that environment shapes the man, it is also true that the role of great men is to shape the world.... After each of my numerous meetings with Stroheim, I remember chiefly the impression of a captive chained to his destiny. That is the fate of creators. They become the slaves of their creation. Stroheim's death, as a citizen of a world sprung from his imagination, conformed to the rules he had imagined. His destiny, although his own handiwork, was not within his control, however, and carried him away to a paradise as far from Schönbrunn as from Hollywood or Paris. In this paradise he was to find white-uniformed officers slowly and somberly waltzing to the laments of phantom violins."

As director, he directed his own life as much as he did his films. As actor, it was in his own life that he played his best role. As creative artist, he insisted to the last, even in defeat, on his own "Eppur si muove!"*

— Herman G. Weinberg
November, 1973

*Galileo before the Inquisition, under his breath, "Nevertheless, it *does* move!"

CREDITS

Adolph Zukor and Jesse Lasky
by arrangement with P. A. Powers
present

The Wedding March

In its entirety
a von Stroheim creation*

Story and Continuity by
Erich von Stroheim and Harry Carr
Directed by Erich von Stroheim

Settings and Design . . . . Erich von Stroheim
Captain Richard Day

Military consultants . . . . Count Albert Conti
D. R. O. Hatswell, R.N.

Assistant directors. . . . . Eddy Sowders
Louis Germonprez

Second assistant directors . . . . Eddie Malone
Art Jell

Special historical consultant . . . . Archduke Leopold of Hapsburg

Photography . . . . Hal Mohr
B. Sorenson

Musical score (synchronized) . . . . J. S. Zamecnik
Louis de Francesco

Musical arrangements . . . . John M. Leipold
Victor Young

*Of this screen credit, which appears in the film, it could be said, ''In its entirety it was, it was!''

Cast

Prince Ottokar Ladislaus von Wildeliebe-Rauffenburg,
    His Majesty's Chamberlain, Lord Steward, General
    of Cavalry and Captain of all Guards . . . . George Fawcett

Princess Maria Immaculata von Wildeliebe-Rauffenburg,
    his wife, and former Lady-in-Waiting to H.I.M. the
    Empress Elizabeth. . . . . Maude George

Prince Nicholaus ("Nicki") Erhart Hans Karl Maria
    von Wildeliebe-Rauffenburg, their son, and First Lieutenant
    in His Majesty's Lifeguard Mounted . . . . Erich von Stroheim

Maid to Prince Nicki . . . . Lucille Van Lent

Fortunat Schweisser, corn-plaster magnate ("Red
    Raven Cornplasters, one crown at all drugstores") . . . . George Nichols

Cecelia, his limping daughter . . . . Zasu Pitts

Maid to Cecelia . . . . Lurie Weiss

Martin Schrammel, violinist at the *Heuriger*, "Zum Alten
    Apfelbaum," in Nussdorf. . . . . Cesare Gravina

Mitzi, his daughter, harpist at the *Heuriger* . . . . Fay Wray

Katerina, his wife, hostess at the *Heuriger* . . . . Dale Fuller

Anton Eberle, proprietor of the *Heuriger* . . . . Hughie Mack

Johann Adalbert ("Schani") Eberle, his son, butcher
    and the fiancé of Mitzi . . . . Matthew Betz

Emperor Franz Josef . . . . Anton Wawerka

Navratil, valet to Prince Nicki . . . . Sidney Bracey

Mountain guide idiot . . . . Danny Hoy

H.I.H. Archduke Leopold Salvator . . . . Don Ryan

Officers of the Imperial Guard . . . . Captain Peter von
    Hartmann, Carey Harrison, Schumann-Heink, Harry Reinhardt, Wilhelm von Brincken,
    Captain John S. Peters

The Setting: Vienna, Nussdorf, the Tyrol
The Time: The Spring and Summer of 1914

Released October 1928 by Paramount Famous Lasky Corporation

Shooting Time: 9 months (plus 4 months for writing the script and cutting Part One)
Production Cost: $900,000, according to von Stroheim; $1,125,000, according to P. A. Powers.
Length: Part One (released version) — 10,400 feet
Part Two (briefly released) — 7,000 feet

Reduced from 200,000 feet shot and 50,000 feet edited

PRODUCTION STILLS

Hearts and hopes high — P. A. (Pat) Powers, the film's financial backer,
and the director pose for a publicity shot on the eve of the start of shooting.
(The lady is unidentified.)

Rehearsing the first exterior scene, the Corpus Christi procession before the
Cathedral of St. Stephen's. Here the military police are being drilled by the director.

The Emperor's Lifeguards Mounted receive their instructions from the director,
who will join them as their squadron leader when the scene is shot.

"What is he doing with the Grand Cross of the Order of St. Stephen?"
demands the director of Albert Conti, one of his technical assistants.

The director, dressed for the scene, takes time out to pose with his cameraman, Hal Mohr, and Mr. Mohr's new bride, who has come to visit the set.

Before shooting of the Corpus Christi scene starts, the director poses for a publicity
shot in front of a mock-up of the façade of the cathedral.

Shooting the Corpus Christi scene during which Prince Nicki (second plumed helmet from the left under the sun umbrella) meets Mitzi among the crowd gathered to watch the pageant.

Some days later, before shooting the scene of the arrival of the Emperor
in his state carriage in the Corpus Christi ceremony, Mr. Powers (second from left),
Jesse Lasky, mogul at Paramount, through whom the film is committed for release,
and the director pose for another publicity still.

Top: Many months later, in the Sierras, the company pauses during the shooting of
the wedding trip of Prince Nicki and Princess Cecelia to the Rauffenburg chateau in
the Tyrolean Alps . . . the opening scene of Part Two. *Bottom:* In the Sierras, filming
Schani's chase after Prince Nicki. Matthew Betz as Schani (second from left, front)
and the director (fourth from right).

After 9 months, Powers has ordered shooting stopped, with the film not quite
finished. Now starts the task of editing the immense footage (some 200,000 feet).
The director at the viewer in his cutting room.

The director with his chief cutter, Frank Hull, discusses the best way to edit a scene.
The shelves contain indexed rolls of film of the various scenes shot for the picture.

The director, Mr. Hull and two other cutters discuss the ''cinema bed of Procrustes''
that the long film will have to fit — or else it will be taken away from them,
as indeed it was. Was the sign above their heads a bad omen?

84

PRINCIPAL CHARACTERS

Prince Nicki (Erich von Stroheim)

Mitzi (Fay Wray)

87

Prince Ottokar (George Fawcett)

Princess Maria (Maude George)

88

Anton Eberle (Hughie Mack)

Schani Eberle (Matthew Betz)

89

Mitzi's mother (Dale Fuller)

Cecelia (Zasu Pitts)

Emperor Franz Josef (Anton Wawerka)

Mitzi's father (Cesare Gravina)

Cecelia's father, Schweisser (George Nichols)

NOTES ON THE
RECONSTRUCTION
OF THE FILM

Those portions of the captions in italics are either verbatim from the subtitles in the released version of Part One, from the original screenplay, or quotations from other sources. In Part Two, italics indicate captions drawn either from the original screenplay or from other sources.

All stills of Part One that were parts of scenes deleted from the version of *The Wedding March* put into general release are appropriately identified by

---
CUT

Since the whole of Part Two is, as far as can be ascertained, lost,* the individual stills illustrating it are, therefore, not further identified as being missing from the lost film.

The entire sequence in Part One of the Corpus Christi procession was photographed in Technicolor, although the stills illustrating this sequence are in black-and-white.

The version of the original screenplay fol-

*According to Henri Langlois, curator of the Cinémathèque Française, the one print of Part Two known to exist was destroyed in a fire that occurred in a blockhouse where it had been inadvertently stored by a functionary of the archive, said blockhouse being a temporary repository for prints of films in transit from one place to another. The accident occurred five days after the death of Stroheim on May 12, 1957. Since the director had forbidden Langlois to show the film because the editing was not by him, crucial scenes were missing, and the film was unfinished, anyway, it became a *film maudit*. Langlois is convinced "il est mort volontairement," that "it died voluntarily"; in short, that the print "committed suicide" on the funeral pyre in the blockhouse. Out of humiliation, out of affront at its dismemberment, out of shame for having been disowned and not wishing to outlive its creator. A true suttee. It is such flights that make Henri Langlois the foremost film curator in the world.

Or, to quote from *The Wedding March* itself: "There is no such thing as accident. It is Fate — misnamed."

lowed in establishing the sequence of the stills of Parts One and Two is P. A. Powers's (the film producer's) own copy, acquired by the author, as were the stills, from Mr. Powers's estate.

Four versions appear to have preceded the released version:

— First cut by von Stroheim and Frank E. Hull, his personal cutter, of Part One: 25,795 feet.

— Second cut by Josef von Sternberg, at the request of Paramount and with the approval of von Stroheim, according to Sternberg: 17,993 feet.

— Third cut (still of Part One only) by Julian Johnston: 11,147 feet.

— Fourth cut: 11,062 feet.

— Fifth and final cut: 10,852 feet, released on 14 reels accompanied by 14 discs of the synchronized musical score.

— Part Two, first cut by Stroheim: 22,484 feet.

— Second cut by Sternberg: 10,789 feet.*

— Third cut: approximately 7,000 feet, of which some 2,000 feet constituted a reprise of footage from Part One to make of the unfinished Part Two a "separate whole film, complete in itself."

*These footages are from a cutting dossier on the film salvaged by me from the Powers estate and given to the archives of the Cinémathèque Française.

PART ONE
THE WEDDING MARCH

J. S. Zamecnik

Slow Waltz

From

" THE WEDDING MARCH "

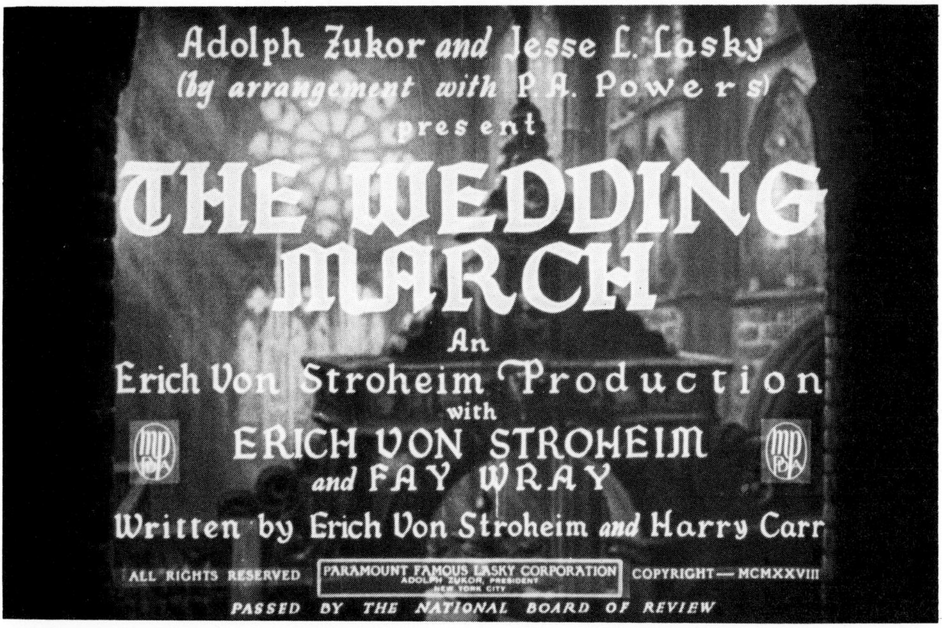
Adolph Zukor and Jesse L. Lasky
(by arrangement with P.A. Powers)
present
THE WEDDING MARCH
An
Erich Von Stroheim Production
with
ERICH VON STROHEIM
and FAY WRAY
Written by Erich Von Stroheim and Harry Carr
ALL RIGHTS RESERVED
PARAMOUNT FAMOUS LASKY CORPORATION
ADOLPH ZUKOR, PRESIDENT
NEW YORK CITY
COPYRIGHT — MCMXXVIII
PASSED BY THE NATIONAL BOARD OF REVIEW

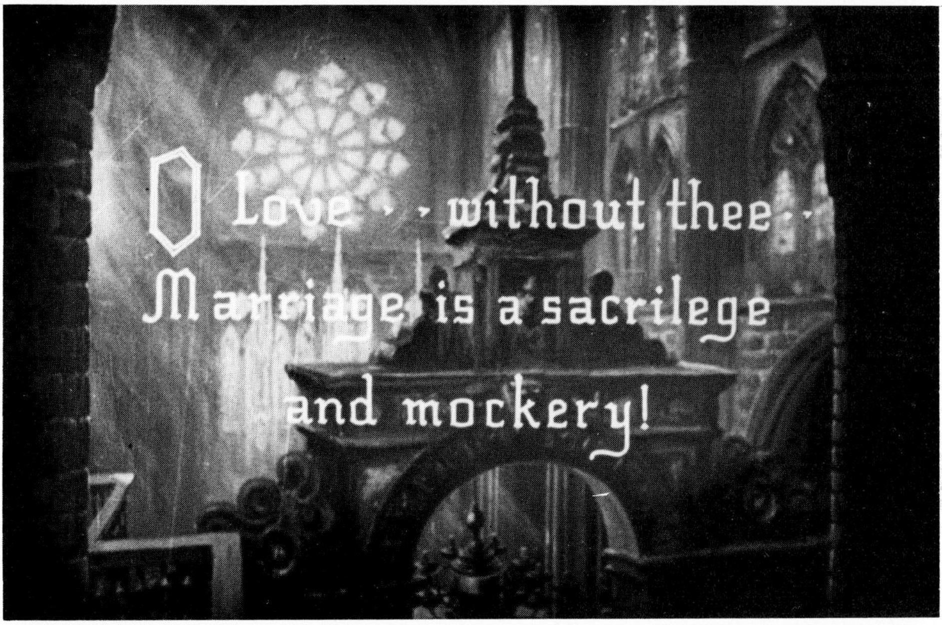
O Love - - without thee - -
Marriage is a sacrilege
and mockery!

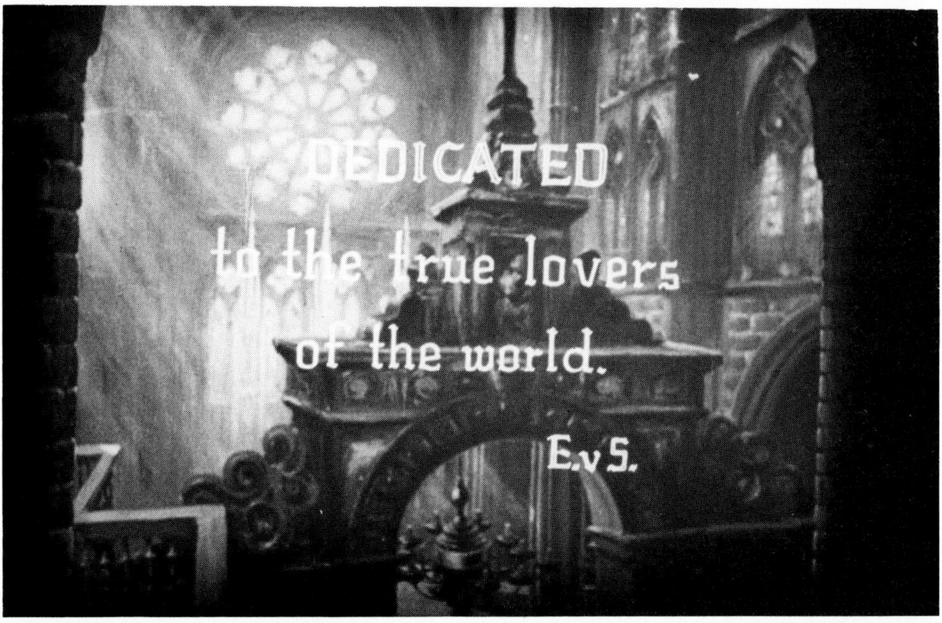
DEDICATED
to the true lovers
of the world.
E.v S.

Vienna, Anno Domini 1914 . . . under the benign reign of His Royal and Imperial Majesty, Franz Josef of Hapsburg, Emperor of Austria, King of Bohemia, Apostolic King of Hungary, King of Jerusalem, Defender of the Catholic Faith (Anton Wawerka). *(The statuette is that of the late Empress Elizabeth.)*

It is the morning of Corpus Christi Day. Her Highness, the Princess Maria Immaculata von Wildeliebe-Rauffenburg, former Lady-in-Waiting to Her Imperial Majesty, the Empress Elizabeth, awakes. (Maude George)

The morning cigar and the usual contemptuous look at her husband,
vis-à-vis in the adjoining bed.

His Highness, Prince Ottokar Ladislaus von Wildeliebe-Rauffenburg, His Majesty's Chamberlain, Lord Steward
General of Cavalry and Captain of All Guards, returns the look. (George Fawcett

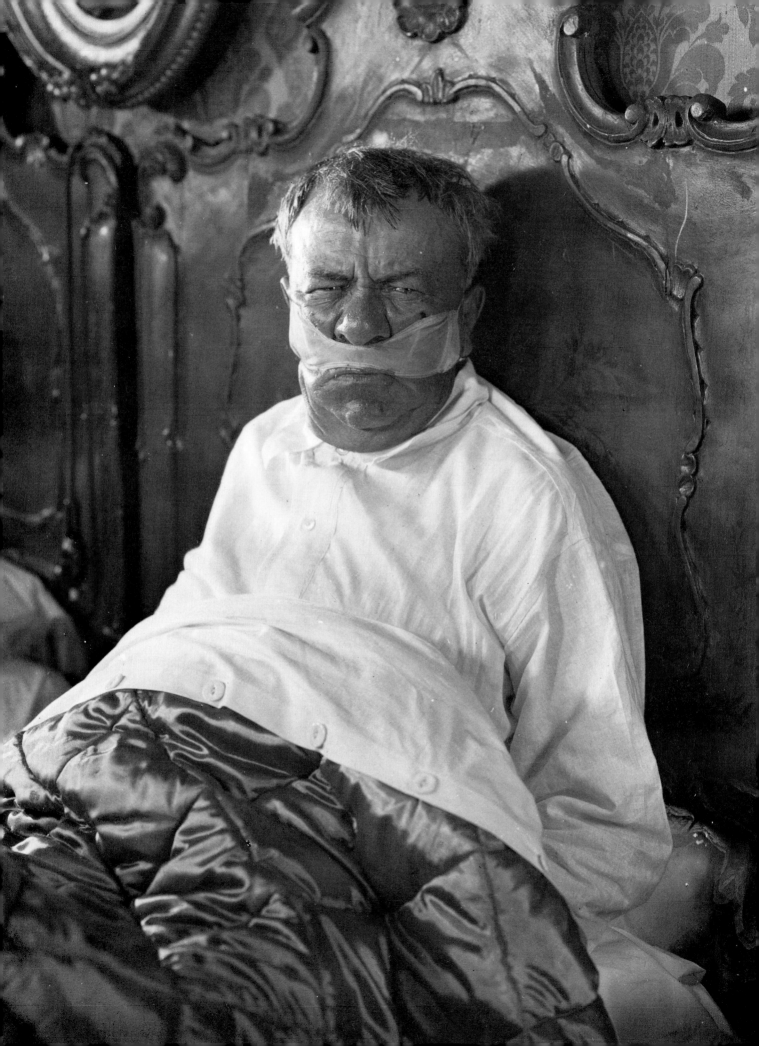

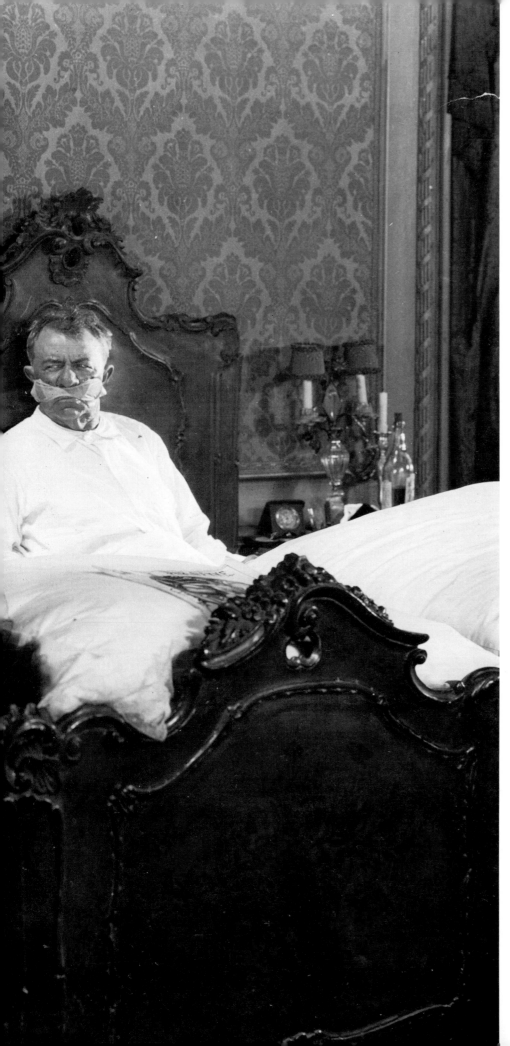

"*Well, come on, say it!*" says the Prince. "*You ugly old fool!*" says the Princess. "*You should see yourself,*" says the Prince; "*it's pitiful!*" (Detail: The bridal wreath over the bed in "Greed" is echoed here between the twin beds.)

"It's Corpus Christi Day, Your Highness," says Prince Nicki's personal maid, waking him. *The "love child" of this ideal, blissful union slumbered still.*

His Highness, Nicholaus Ehrhart Hans Karl Maria Prince von Wildeliebe-Rauffenburg . . .

. . . His Majesty's Chamberlain and First Lieutenant of the Imperial and Royal Lifeguards Mounted (Erich von Stroheim).

His "eye-opener" — sherry and egg.

. . . ''to the nines'' . . .

"Anybody got any money?"

Five years before, Karamzin was cadging money from his maid, Marushka,
in *Foolish Wives* (not to mention from Mrs. Hughes, the American ambassador's wife)
—here Prince Nicki is still carrying on the old tradition of
Stroheim's male protagonists.

1012-52

Ritual of dressing — with complications: an irksome corn soothed by the
ubiquitous corn-plaster palliative of one Herr Schweisser, corn-plaster magnate,
who will play an important role in the Wildeliebe-Rauffenburg story.

Turned down for a touch by Papa, Nicki is told by him to *"Blow your brains out —
or — marry money."* Nicki decides to try Mama.

"How much does the hand-kiss cost this morning?"

"No joking, Mother — I'm in a terrible hole!"

"Stop your poker and your expensive girlies . . .," says Mama, *". . . or . . . marry money."*

To which Nicki wearily agrees, "*But meanwhile, if you can let me have a little . . .*"

Then, *Corpus Christi* — *the greatest religious and military celebration of the year.*

"Just stick around me, folks!" says Schani (Matthew Betz) *"That's the truth,"*
says his father, *"My boy always gets the best places."* (Hughie Mack)
"You said it, Herr Eberle," says Mitzi's mother. *"The girl who gets him is lucky!"* (Dale Fuller)

"Are you harpin' again on the same old thing?" says Mitzi (Fay Wray).

"Saphead! You're goin' to lose
e best chance you'll ever have!"

Arrival of the Emperor in his state coach . . .

Prince Nicki standing duty in the Stefansplatz before the Cathedral . . .

. . . salutes his Emperor.

Inside the Cathedral, before the altar, kneels the Emperor in his role as
Guardian of the Faith.

"Move back . . . move back!"

"Ain't we got no right to see nothin' a-tall?"

A better view

Lunch . . .

And then it happened . . . Mitzi looks up . . .

Who ever loved who loved not at first sight?

Inside the Cathedral in the front pew are the Wildeliebe-Rauffenburgs,
with their dual crests emblazoned below them . . .

. . . while nearby, also participating in the High Mass, are rich Herr Schweisser (George Nichols) and his clubfooted daughter, Cecelia (Zasu Pitts).

Ambitious to make a fortuitous marriage between his daughter and the son of the broke Wildeliebe-Rauffenburgs, he looks anxiously at them . . .

The Mass is over and the celebrants begin to emerge from the Cathedral . . .

A salute of rifles in the Emperor's honor frightens Prince Nicki's horse,
who rears up and knocks Mitzi down.

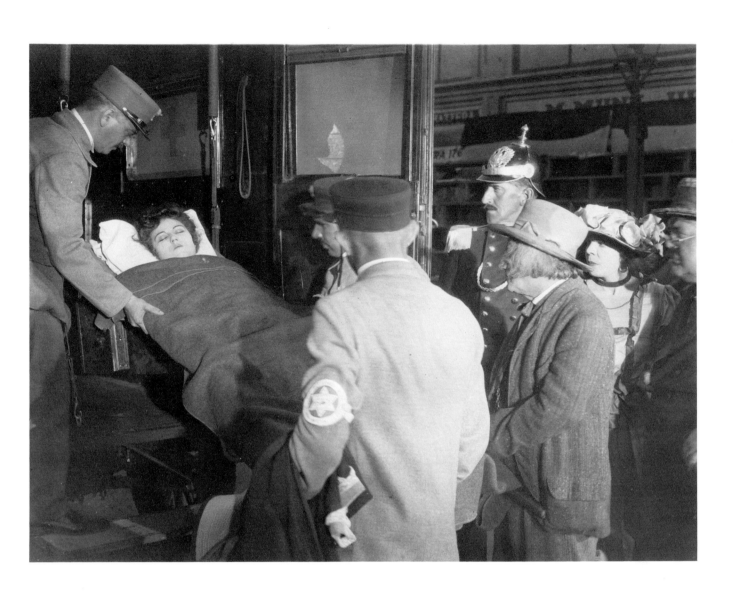

And then the procession — the procession which Mitzi had waited so long to see.

There is no such thing as accident. It is Fate — misnamed.

Prince Nicki greets Mitzi's father *(Cesare Gravina)* in the hospital room
the Prince has provided for her. *"How are you?"* he asks, and
presents her with a sumptuous box of chocolates.

Then, dreamy Nussdorf . . .

Wiener Schwalben . . . Vienna Swallows

After the guests had gone . . . "You owe me a kiss, Mitzi — you blew out the match."

*"Our beautiful 'Blue Danube'... Down there the 'Danube Maids' come to the shore —
sometimes... an' to see them means happiness — an' luck — and love!...
I never saw them an' I suppose I never will, but I'm satisfied just so I don't see
the 'Iron Man'!"*

"What do they say about him?" "They say some nights he comes to life—an' drags away a Danube Maid . . ."

". . . an' to the ones who see him . . . comes Sorrow . . . Grief . . . an' Death!"

"You believe that, Mitzerl?" She nods. *"It's nothing but the people's fancies,"* says Nicki.

After Nicki has gone . . .

Mitzi's mother tells Schani of the attentions being paid Mitzi by the Prince. *"He believes in workin' fast!"*

Schani now realizes he has a rival.

Then, in that little crooked house . . . in that little crooked street.

CUT

At the peepholes . . .

What they see — Prince Ottokar at dominoes with the girls . . . the director here
outwits the censors at their own game.

"A kiss all around and then I leave you," says Nicki. "Tonight I crave
apple blossoms. I'm going to meet a real nice girl." "At this hour of the morning?"
"It's when her parents snore the loudest!"

After a night of spree
I come under your window
As to an altar.
        —Old Flamenco Song

"I was afraid you wouldn't come," says Mitzi. *"I was on duty,"* replies Nicki,
"and couldn't get away."

Old Schweisser's corn-plasters come in handy to soothe Prince Ottokar's burning corn . . .

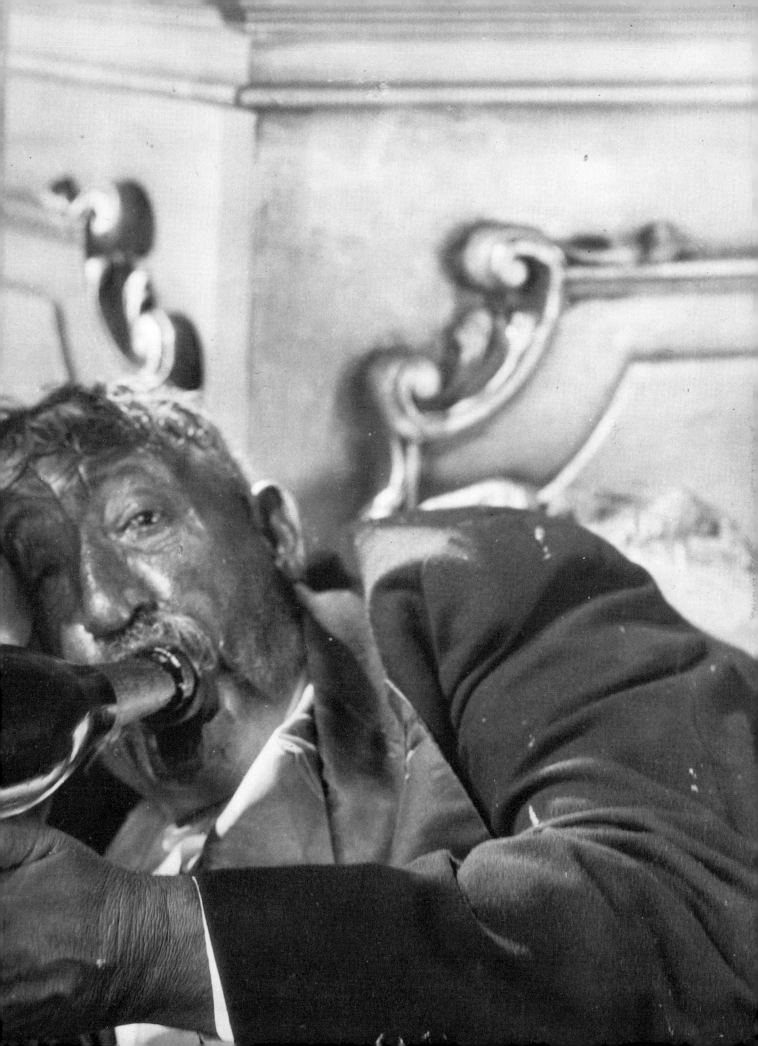

"Now listen . . . Highness . . . I . . . h-have . . . a . . . p-proposition," says Schweisser. "Y-you h-have a n-nice son . . . a-an' n-no m-money . . ."

". . . a-an' I h-have . . . a n-nice g-girl . . . a-an' l-lots o-o' m-money . . . understand??"

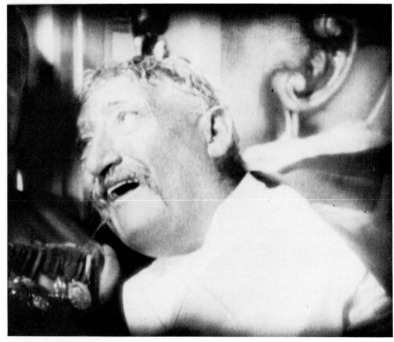

"I-I'll fix your s-son u-up right . . . u-understand?"
"How much do I get?"
"Five Hunder' Thousan' Kronen!"
"How much??"
"One million kronen!"

The pact is sealed. The cynical opportunism of the upper middle class and
the aristocracy as depicted in Hogarth's "Marriage à la Mode" finds its echo here
. . . a betrothal serving only the vanity and avarice of the parents.

Mitzi sees the "Iron Man" . . .

1012:8

It was mid-morning before Schweisser dragged himself home to face his daughter.

"I was with His Highness Prince von Wildeliebe-Rauffenburg . . . and we have arranged for you and his son, Prince Nicki, to get married."
"But I have never even met the Prince . . . how could he be in love with me?"
"You have twenty millions . . . and love will come, in time."

"Princess Cecelia . . . won't that sound nice?" "A limping Princess!"

"Did it ever occur to you that I might be in love with somebody else?"
says Nicki to his father, when informed of the pact with Schweisser.

"You in love?" says Prince Ottokar. *"You idiot!"*

"Of course, you two wouldn't know, but some people do fall in love . . . really!"

"But marriage is one thing," says Nicki's mother, *"and love another . . . n'est-ce pas, Ottokar?"*

"How dare he talk to me like that?" says Nicki.
"But Nicki . . . this would mean so much money," says his mother.
"How much?" "A huge fortune!"

"Seems to me," answers Nicki, *"that girl limps — on both legs."*

Confess yourself to Heaven . . . repent what is past . . . avoid what is to come.

191

Pax tecum. . . .

Then Nature mourned . . . . . . the birds were hushed . . . . . . for weeks it rained and rained and rained. . . . On the eve of his marriage to Cecelia, Nicki comes to say goodbye to Mitzi.

Next morning, Schani reminds Mitzi that her Prince Charming is getting married at St. Stephen's that afternoon. . . .

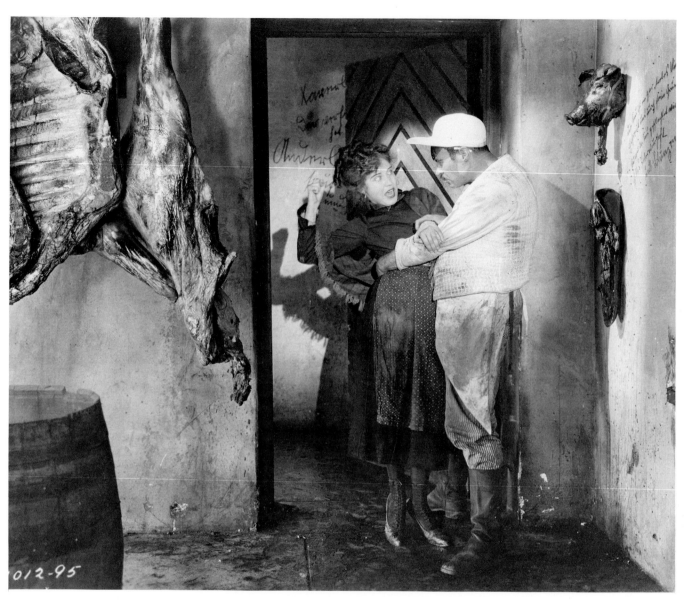

. . . and when Mitzi says she still loves Nicki and always will,
Schani loses patience with her. . . .

"I'll kill that damned sow-dog when he comes out of church today!"

Mitzi arrives at the Cathedral. . . .

". . . until death do you part . . ."

Te Deum laudamus. . . .

209

Mitzi looks for Schani. . . .

. . . she sees him . . . and runs to tell him she will marry him if he will spare Nicki. . . .

The Prince and Princess Nicholaus von Wildeliebe-Rauffenburg,
having walked down the aisle to the "Wedding March," now prepare to begin their
journey through life together.

213

"Say your last 'Ta-Ta' to him!"

"Nicki . . . who was that sweet girl in tears . . . and that awful looking man?"
"I . . . I never saw them before."
"How beautiful these apple blossoms are. . . . won't they always remind you . . . ?"
"Yes . . . always!"

PART TWO
THE HONEYMOON

OPENING SEQUENCE FROM THE ORIGINAL SCREENPLAY

FADE IN

L S   On wonderful landscape with mountains in background covered in eternal snow, but partially covered with fog. High fir trees in the foreground. A roadway leads through these trees toward background—in foreground is a four-foot boulder wall with highly impressive iron gate. On arch of gate is deer head with eighteen prongs and the Wildeliebe-Rauffenburg crest underneath in iron—on right-hand side of wall is small caretaker's house in Tyrolean style with rocks on roof, etc. It is raining and the trees and mountains are half in fog and the landscape looks dreary, cold and unfriendly. The doorkeeper, his wife and idiot son, a few peasants and children, all in overcoats, are at the gate. A closed carriage with driver and footman in livery drives into scene at high speed. The people at gate bare their heads and bow. The left rear wheel flies off the carriage and the carriage falls on left rear end to ground. Driver and footman jump off. Peasants and doorkeeper run to carriage.

M C U   Inside of carriage. Cecelia in corner of side from which wheel fell off, with Nicki almost on top of her through the impact and the sudden fall. He is in almost the identical position as he was with Mitzi so often. Cecelia is terribly frightened and Nicki asks her quickly and in an agitated way whether she is hurt. She says, "No," but one can see that she feels almost ill through shock. Door is opened by footman and driver.

M S   From left of carriage. Driver and footman help Nicki out, who in turn, helps Cecelia. He supports her and very attentively tries to comfort her. She tries so hard to be brave, but her lips twitch and her eyes fill with tears. In spite of this, she tells Nicki that everything is all right.

M C U   Nicki looks absent-mindedly at carriage.

SHOT   FROM HIS ANGLE of carriage with wheel off.

                                                    LAP OUT

LAP INTO

M C U   Scene with carriage from Mitzi's apple orchard in identical position; branches with apple blossoms over them.

                                                    LAP OUT

LAP BACK

MED SHT   Prince Nicki's carriage with people busy around it.

B T   Nicki—he looks almost sadly in direction of carriage. CAMERA MOVES BACK UNTIL Cecelia is in also and then CAMERA MOVES STILL further back. Driver and footman enter scene and tell Nicki they cannot fix wheel. He looks toward carriage. CAMERA MOVES farther back until everybody is in. Just then another carriage drives in background of Nicki's carriage and halts. They are the personal servants of Nicki and Cecelia. They jump out and join the group. Nicki sees the other carriage and quickly decides to go with Cecelia in the servants' carriage. He quickly supports Cecelia to servants' carriage in background—she carries cardboard box with bridal bouquet. He helps Cecelia in, who is still very much frightened, but tries bravely to smile. He enters also. Driver and footman jump on box and carriage drives out, while rest of people stand around broken carriage looking after the departing Nicki.

LAP OUT

LAP INTO

M C U   Of old Prophet-like man with snow-white hair, on crutches looking after departing carriage, slowly shaking his head. He takes the pipe out of his mouth, spits, then says:

TITLE: "—A wheel off!—"
He finishes and continues:

TITLE: "—don't mean nothin' good!—"
He finishes.

LAP OUT

LAP INTO

L S   Front with main entrance of castle with steps leading up to it. Great door, around which stand in groups the servants of Nicki, in their national gala costumes, but with capes, coats, etc., and umbrellas. It is, of course, raining. Around front entrance are temporary decorations of garlands and festoons of fir branches and bunting and a large sign: *Willkommen*. The bunting and flags are soaking wet and dripping. The carriage drives in, footman dismounts and helps Nicki and Cecelia out.

MED SHT   Cecelia stepping out, helped by Nicki—she is dressed in her black traveling dress with crêpe on her hat. She limps as she walks. Hangs rather heavily on Nicki's arm (still carrying box).

M S   People. They look at each other, nudge each other discreetly and whisper.

B T S   All in. Superintendent of estate with hat in hand bids the Prince and·his young wife welcome in the name of the servants. Nicki shakes hands with him and so does Cecelia. A little girl in peasant costume carrying a bouquet of Alpine roses and edelweiss in paper cuff, steps up to Cecelia and hands her the flowers. The chief forester then turns toward the servants and with his hat in the air, he cheers. They all cheer, waving their hats. Nicki and Cecelia enter the house.

LAP OUT

LAP INTO

M S   CAMERA ON PA'M moves back through door of entrance into hall. Cecelia and Nicki about to enter. Their personal servants and the Superintendent behind them. As Cecelia steps over door threshold, she slips and falls—dropping box, which breaks, revealing her bridal bouquet—Nicki starts to pick it up—she tries to hide it from him. Nicki picks her up with mixed feelings of embarrassment, sympathy and pity since everybody has seen it and since he knows that it is an ill omen. She did not hurt herself, but she is very embarrassed and almost cries. She looks with tear-dimmed eyes at Nicki, in a heartbreaking pathetic way. He looks a little out of sorts with her, but controls himself before the people looking on. He smiles faintly. They start walking toward camera as they enter.

M C U   Three old hags among the servants—the oldest says:

TITLE: "—Sure—as I'm a hundred years old!—"
She finishes and continues:

TITLE: "—Grief!—"
She finishes and continues:

TITLE: "—Sickness!—"
She finishes and continues:

TITLE: "—Death!—"
She finishes.

The carriage taking Prince Nicki and Cecelia to the Wildeliebe-Rauffenburg chateau
in the Tyrolean Alps breaks down as one wheel comes off — a bad omen.

Prince Nicki and Cecelia ponder their next move.

Another carriage with some of the family retainers rescues them.
Prince Nicki and Cecelia get in . . .

. . . and off they go.

Arrival of the royal couple at the chateau being greeted by the servants attached to the manor house.

The superintendent of the estate bids the Prince and his young wife welcome.

A little girl carrying a bouquet of Alpine roses and edelweiss greets them, too.

The ritual of offering bread and salt — symbol of hospitality — to the new member of the family.

A guest is in the house — God is in the house.

How long, how long, in infinite Pursuit
Of This and That endeavour and dispute?
Better be merry with the fruitful Grape
Than sadden after none, or bitter, Fruit.

And if the Wine you drink, the Lip you press,
End in Nothing all Things end in — Yes —
Then fancy while Thou art, Thou art but what
Thou shalt be — Nothing — Thou shalt not be less.

— *Rubáiyát*

''Dreimal musst Du es sagen,'' says Goethe in *Faust*. ''Three times you must say it.'' The script called for three omens of bad luck which pursued Cecelia — the broken carriage wheel, the rain on her arrival (omitted by the director), and her stumbling over the threshold.

Wedding of Mitzi and Schani.

*"Do you, Johann Adalbert Eberle, take the honorable Virgin,
Maria Francesca Schrammel, for your lawful wedded wife?"*
(The gargoyles of their respective families are right out of *Greed*.)

Mitzi faints.

That does it for Schani. He vows that this time he really *will* kill Nicki.

Wedding night, holy night.

Cecelia, unaccustomed to champagne,
is made dizzy by it.

Nicki helps her, sympathetically.

"Don't you hate me—that you had to marry me . . ."

'. . . just to get some of father's stupid money?''

"To be here, with just me . . . alone . . . poor little limping me!"

As Nicki carries his bride up to their bedroom they encounter one of the servants, also just married, taking *his* bride to a bedroom in the servants' quarters.

"The champagne tickles my nose," she says. Then, *"I can be as gay . . . and giddy . . . as your gay ladies . . ."*

"I could learn fast, if you'll only teach me," she says.
"I'll do anything that your gay ladies do . . . anything!"

Nicki makes a move to begin to undress her. . . .

(Note portrait of "big brother," Emperor Franz Josef, overlooking the bed.)

Cecelia, to distract him, points to her bridal bouquet on the night-table. ''They're still fresh,'' she says. . . .

''If they'd only last forever!''

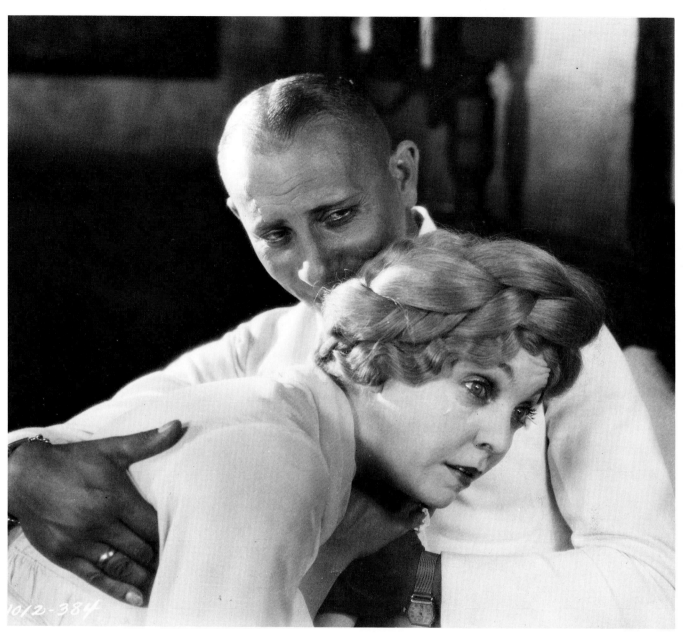

Which was the wrong thing for her to say, as Nicki is reminded of Mitzi and, after brushing her cheek with his lips, he tells her she must be tired and bids her goodnight.

Cecelia futilely regards her honeymoon nightgown. . . .

. . . then bitterly begins to tear it . . .

. . . until it is in shreds, after which she cries
herself to sleep.

Next morning, Nicki is off to his hunting lodge for some shooting.

1012-423

Cecelia tearfully bids him goodbye, after saying how lonesome she will be.

"Goodbye, my love, goodbye . . .," she says. . . .

"... and good-luck!" Which startles them, as it is a bad omen to wish a hunter good luck.

Schani has arrived at the mountain villa of the Wildeliebe-Rauffenburgs where
Cecelia and Nicki are honeymooning — led to it by an idiot guide, seen here with him.

A nameless fear suddenly possesses Cecelia inside, in the chapel to which
she has gone to pray for her and Nicki's safety.

Schani now tells the idiot guide the purpose of his visit, that he is after Prince Nicki.
They seal their conspiracy in Schani's bottle of whiskey.

"... love ye your enemies, and do good, and lend, hoping for nothing again;
and your reward shall be great ... be ye therefore merciful, as your Father also is merciful. ..."

—St. Luke

Inside, Schani demands to know where the master of the house is . . .

. . . and forces the houseman to tell him that the Prince has left for
his hunting lodge on the ridge above.

The idiot guide gives Schani directions to the lodge and they part here,
where shepherdesses rest at a wayside shrine.

Nicki and his entourage pause on the way up as dusk is closing in on them.

The slow, arduous climb is over, the men have reached the hunting lodge on the ridge above,
where "Auf der Alm da gibts kein Sünd" — "On the Alps there is no sin."
They laugh at the plaque with those burned-in words nailed to the hut.

Meanwhile Cecelia, inconsolable, has persuaded the servants to put guides
at her disposal to bring her to her husband.

One of the mountain guides points out that dark is closing in,
the climb is long and treacherous, and that they had better be on their way.

Mitzi, also fearful for Nicki's safety, and knowing of Schani's threat really to kill him this time, reaches a wayside inn and asks directions to the chateau of the Wildeliebe-Rauffenburgs. . . . She describes Schani to them . . . have they seen him?

The idiot guide says, yes, he has seen him, and he knows just where he is.
Mitzi engages him to lead her.

Cecelia has made it, with the help of her guides.

Mitzi pauses at the same shrine that earlier Nicki and his men did,
and prays that she will find her way to him in time.

Alpha and omega. . . . Mitzi's love for Nicki is confronted by the idiot guide's lust for her.

And Schani lusts to kill Nicki. . . .

Cecelia, now safely in the hut, has called Nicki, and he comes to her.

"Don't you feel something?" asks Cecelia, frightened. And when Nicki replies,
"It's only the lightning outside, the thunder and hail," Cecelia insists, "There is something — and it's coming nearer!"

Schani, hearing a commotion, raises his lamp to see. . . .

Mitzi and Schani confront each other.

But Schani will not be deterred from his purpose. . . .

. . . to kill Nicki. Cecelia, seeing his shadow through the window,
again calls out to Nicki and as he comes rushing in she gets up and throws herself
in front of him at the moment that Schani fires . . . hitting Cecelia.

Nicki orders a posse of mountain men to go after Schani. . . .

The posse is given instructions by their leader.

"He that digs a pit shall fall into it."
— *Ecclesiastes*

A doctor and priest from the valley below have been sent for by Nicki,
and now Mitzi is there, too.

Cecelia has been mortally wounded. . . . .

Nicki and Mitzi confront each other.

"Did you get hurt, Nicki?" asks Cecelia.

Cecelia dies.

The ecclesiasts and doctor prepare to return to the valley.
(Detail: Over the door are inscribed the letters "C + M + B," standing for
"Die Drei Heiligen" — the three holy ones — Caspar, Melchior and Balthazar —
the three kings who were guided by a star to where the Christ Child lay.
A Central European motto inscribed over doorways of the faithful.)

". . . and forgive us our trespasses as we forgive those who trespass against us . . ."

Parting of Mitzi and Nicki . . .

303

"... and deliver us from evil. ..."

Mitzi returns to Vienna, to her parents . . . and tells them of the death of Cecelia and Schani . . .

. . . and begs Schani's father for forgiveness.

An evening, shortly after, *chez eux* at the chateau of the Wildeliebe-Rauffenburgs.
A fire is crackling in the hearth, Princess Maria is having a glass of champagne,
and Nicki is brooding by the fire.

They are joined by Prince Ottokar.

Princess Maria knows what's eating her son . . . a mother knows
the secret places of her child's heart . . .

Still, she has to say it, so: *"Well, Nicki, your matrimonial venture was a huge success, n'est-ce pas?"* She pauses. *"The eternal problem of the exchequer brilliantly solved forever!"* Again she pauses. *"Now you're free to go back to your girlies . . . everything's lovely!"*

"Yes, indeed," says Nicki, looking at her with withering scorn. *"Very lovely!"* Shocked beyond anything he can say at her callousness, he makes a sweeping gesture at the family crest over the fireplace. *"Pro Gloria Dei, Patriae et Familiae!"* he intones, *"For the Glory of God, Country and Family — especially the family!"*

Nicki's contempt is not lost on his parents. *"Why this pious horror?"*
says Prince Ottokar. *"I didn't notice that you were dragged screaming to the altar!"*
To which he adds with a sardonic smile, *"I suppose the idea of money
never entered your head, eh?"*

It was apple-blossom time that summer in Vienna — in the winegardens and
secret bowers of lovers, in the bouquets carried by new brides, and here, in St. Stephen's,
where she was married, adorning the altar before which Cecelia's coffin now rests.

"I am the Resurrection and the Life. . . ."
And a father weeps at the bier of his child
amid the panoply of a guard of honor,
wreaths and flowers, and ribbons of silk
proclaiming the anguished words,
*"Mea culpa, mea culpa, mea maxima
culpa"* . . . "The sins of the fathers shall be
visited upon their children." . . .

"Forgive us our trespasses as we forgive
those who trespass against us." . . .

But in the end a father is alone with his child, beyond the power of words to comfort,
with only her and his grief. If he had not been so ambitious for her . . . if . . . if . . . !

. . . June passed . . . long weary summer days. . . . then July dragged on to its close. . . .
Nicki comes to visit the wine-garden again . . . to find Mitzi again. . . .

"For Rent"

"For Sale," says the sign on Schani's butcher shop. . . .
"For Sale," too, is the woman who accosts him. . . .

Nicki decides to go in. . . .

. . . gone are the apple-blossoms. . . .

A piece of paper blows against his foot. He looks down and sees that it is a sheet of
music. He picks it up—it is part of the score of "Paradise," the song Mitzi played
the night of their first rendezvous here. . . .

Now there are only ghosts — and not even that — nothing, only desolation. . . .

. . . nothing . . .

"Abfahrt," says the sign, alongside a finger pointing. . . . "Departure." . . .
There's nothing here anymore.

Here production on the film stopped. But the screenplay continued up to the very end, a synopsis of which follows.

Nicki seeks out Mitzi and learns that she has entered a convent to atone for the death of Cecelia, for which she feels responsible.

"Mitzerl," Nicki pleads, "you must leave with me at once—we'll follow spring around the world—I want to see your head framed in apple blossoms again."

"No, Nicki," she says. "I haven't found my peace yet, but I'll pray for it, and I'll pray for you, too, Nicki." Then, "Let's say that between us it was only a dream—but such a beautiful dream! Oh Nicki," she cries out and throws herself in his arms for a last embrace. "Whenever you see apple blossoms"—she smiles through her tears—"think of me."

Nicki returns to Madame Rosa's to forget, to find oblivion. "Well, well," she says, seeing him enter unsteadily, "the prodigal returns!"

The Emperor's study at Schönbrunn. Around his desk are his staff, ministers and generals, waiting for his signature on the declaration of war against Serbia. The assassination of the Archduke Ferdinand at Sarajevo had already taken place. If Russia would back Serbia, Germany would back Austria. The military was champing at the bit: They'd been waiting for this opportunity a long time. But the Emperor drops his pen; he can't sign. From behind a portiere in back of the Emperor a mailed fist comes out and in double exposure we see the Iron Man make his appearance. He takes up the pen and puts it in the Emperor's hand and together they both sign it.

Back at Madame Rosa's, Nicki is the top man on the totem pole of a bucket brigade which is passing coolers of champagne forward, hand to hand, until they reach him. He breaks each bottle's neck off on the edge of a bronze tub on a raised dais and empties the bottle in it. Soon the tub is filled. A naked girl is brought in and dumped in the tub. At that instant, and again in double exposure, the Iron Man stalks into the room amid the revelers, stops abruptly and dissolves out. Everyone freezes for a moment, exchanges looks, then rushes to the windows. From the outside we see them at the windows looking down at newsboys in the street shouting, "Extra! Extra! War Declared! Army and Fleet Mobilized!"

"Forty years I've waited for this!" says an old colonel of hussars, a tear coursing down his grizzled cheek, twirling his mustache.

"Well," says another, giving a last toast, "here's to mud, blood and corruption!"

Consternation all around.

In the street, bugles and drums and military bands pierce the night air. Motorcycles whizz by. Companies of troops pass, the thud of goose-stepping, horses clattering over cobblestones, gun-carriages and caissons rumble by, the crunch of tanks rolling by on their treads, howitzers on caterpillar wheels of tractors roll by, followed by the big mortars, then a long column of infantry, with field kitchens and ambulances bringing up the rear. The muzzles of all the guns are festooned with flowers, people cheer and wave their hats and handkerchiefs at the departing troops, girls and civilians take the arms of the men and walk with them. Everyone is smiling. Some weep.*

*"Stroheim . . . who wrote sound novels in the silent days."—Jean-Luc Godard.

328

In front of St. Stephen's they pass, the cathedral now decorated with bunting of the imperial colors—black and yellow (gold). Once more in double exposure we see the Iron Man, this time on a charger, with drawn broadsword, leading three other horsemen, a white horse on which rides the black hooded figure of Death, wildly playing a violin, then Famine, and finally the specter of Disease. The Four Horsemen of the Apocalypse are loose upon the world again.

A convent on the Serbian border.

At the beginning of the conflict, roving bands of ruffians, deserters, outlaws, malcontents of every stripe, taking advantage of the frenzy that gripped the nation, with its attendant chaos, roamed the countryside, pillaging and looting wherever they could.

A troupe of bandits rides into the area and pulls up before the convent. At their head is a grotesque little hunchback in a hussar's uniform, dress sword, fur shako, dolman cape and all, and wearing thick glasses. He gives orders and his men begin clambering over the convent wall. Screams of the nuns inside are heard. Banging at the front door is another grotesque character, dressed in an old dilapidated uniform of an officer of the Austrian Lifeguard Mounted, three sizes too small for him, dirty white pants, torn epaulettes and a banged-up helmet with some matted remnants of a plume. It's our old friend Schani.*

They break the door down and rush in. There

*Had this ending to the film been shot, the death of Schani at the hands of the posse in the mountains would, of course, have been eliminated in favor of the new end devised by the director for Schani.

follows an orgy of the ruffians and the terrified nuns which is a parody of the orgy at Madame Rosa's bordello. The hunchback leader and Schani sit on the steps of an altar in the chapel, gorging and swilling, as the men dump crucifixes, candelabra and all manner of ecclesiastical gold and silver vessels in a heap on the floor. Then they parade the nuns before them, including the Mother Superior, to choose from. One of the nuns is Mitzi.

Schani stares unbelievingly. Mitzi, too, finds the presence of Schani incredible. For a moment time has stopped for these two—but only for a moment. Schani recovers and lets out with, "Well, what do you know? She and me used to be old sweethearts! . . . Weren't we?" he says, turning to Mitzi. "We came damn' close to marryin'," he continues, "damn' close—" and again turning to Mitzi, "didn't we?" Then, "But today I'm goin' to come a little closer!" Mitzi makes a break for it but Schani grabs her only to find his hold broken by the hunchback. "She's mine!" says the hunchback. In a moment the two are stalking each other, the hunchback with a drawn kriss and Schani with a long butcher knife, drawn from his belt. A circle forms around them. Mitzi is forced by the bandits to watch. In the melee, the Mother Superior has escaped on one of the horses in the courtyard and is riding hard for help. As Schani and the hunchback eye each other for an opening wherein they can deal a lethal blow, a priest attached to the convent prays before a statue of St. Rita: "St. Rita, Saint of the impossible and Advocate of desperate causes . . ." Schani lifts the body of the dead hunchback above him and flings it contemptuously before the altar. Panting but triumphant, he looks at Mitzi.

Now the Mother Superior has come upon the squadron of the 6th Dragoons, Nicki's company, bivouacked by the roadside. She tells them of the invasion of the convent.

Schani grabs two bottles of wine and carries Mitzi upstairs as the bandits cheer.

Nicki and his squadron mount their steeds and gallop toward the convent.

Schani astride a chair guzzling from a bottle, enjoying the suspense while Mitzi prays, *"Pater qui es in coelis, Deus miserere nobis!"* He finishes the bottle, flings it away and gets up. "You was always a good-looker," he says grinning, "but now, in this nun's dress, you sure got me goin'." The dragoons arrive and soon are swarming all over the place. Pandemonium. Shots, screams, scuffles. Schani, not to be cheated again out of his girl, grabs Mitzi but Mitzi brings down on his head a crucifix which he twists out of her arm with a yell of pain. Confrontation of Nicki and Schani in Mitzi's cell. Schani throws himself at his nemesis and Nicki fires. Schani goes down with a bullet in his head, cursing his luck as he falls. Confrontation of Nicki and Mitzi, who has revived from her faint. Nicki holds her. She hesitatingly touches his face and he nods smiling, a smile she now returns. And

again there is no accident, it is fate, misnamed. . . . Mitzi and Nicki are finally married at the altar in the convent, but their happiness is to be short-lived. A dispatch rider comes to Nicki with orders to move up the line. "The Mother Superior has some letters and money for you," says Nicki to Mitzi. "Whatever happens, you're mine now—for always! . . . and forever! . . . If I come out of it," continues Nicki, "you'll be here, waiting for me . . . and if I don't . . . I'll be waiting for you."

"I'll pray God keep you safe for me," says Mitzi; to which Nicki answers, "I doubt your prayers will be heard by the right party." He smiles. "They say the cavalry is in the special care of the Gentleman with the forked tail and the cloven hoofs."

Mitzi smiles wanly. They kiss. The guns are firing. Nicki breaks their kiss to say, "The guns are giving us their blessing."

The blare of bugles rends the air again, signal for the dragoons to mount.

"Well, "says Nicki smiling from his mount, "no one can say we didn't have a lot of music!"

Mitzi waves to him, Nicki salutes her with his saber, and gives the signal to ride on. Across the rude wooden bridge leading away from the convent, the dragoons ride out. In the courtyard Mitzi stands looking after them. Now they're out of sight. Mitzi is crying. Guns are booming. World War I has begun.